Rome. New Architecture

Sebastiano Brandolini

Rome
New Architecture

Foreword by Mosè Ricci

Cover
Richard Meier & Partners
Ara Pacis Museum

Editor
Luca Molinari

Design
Marcello Francone

Editing
Silvia Carmignani

Layout
Paola Ranzini

Translations
Robert Burns for Language
Consulting Congressi S.r.l.,
Milan

First published in Italy
in 2008 by
Skira Editore S.p.A.
Palazzo Casati Stampa
via Torino 61
20123 Milano
Italy
www.skira.net

© Studio Margil – Certosa
di Pavia
© 2008 Skira editore,
Milano

Printed and bound in Italy.
First edition

ISBN: 978-88-6130-534-2

Distributed in North America
by Rizzoli International
Publications, Inc., 300 Park
Avenue South, New York,
NY 10010, USA.
Distributed elsewhere
in the world by Thames
and Hudson Ltd., 181A High
Holborn, London WC1V
7QX, United Kingdom.

This volume would not have been possible without the help of many people who are far more intimately acquainted with Rome than I. In spite of the longstanding passion I have cultivated for Rome and its colours and my ever present desire to return, I always feel like an outsider there. I get the streets mixed up, I continually have to look back at the maps, and this makes me feel pleasantly suspended in the indeterminate and soft quality of its time. What is extraordinary about Rome is that there is always something to discover.

I wish to express my thanks to all the friends, lovers and critics of our capital for their generosity with words and encouragement, and for their hospitality and complicity. I have listed them here in alphabetical order: Pietro Bertelli, Luca Casonato, Claudia Conforti, Clara de la Fuente, Vezio De Lucia, Francesco Ghio, Maurizio Giufré, Guido Incerti, Francesco Nissardi, Lorenzo Piroddi, Aldo Ponis, Luigi Prestinenza Puglisi, Franco Purini, Vittorio Savi, Filippo Trevisani and Riccardo Vannucci. A special thanks goes to Richard Ingersoll, to whom I am linked by a strong bond of friendship, professional esteem and shared viewpoints.

But I dedicate this second volume about the architecture of Italian cities—after the first one, a few years ago, dedicated to Milan—to the memory of Robin Evans, who was my professor at the Architectural Association School of Architecture in London from 1980 to 1982. I still have vivid memories of the time spent with him and of his passion, knowledge and, above all, his keen eye. It is with Bob, before his sudden and untimely death in 1993, that I would have liked to visit this extraordinary and intricate city.

In the end I would like to ask the newly elected mayor, Gianni Alemanno, to refrain from demolishing the white box protecting the Ara Pacis. He should respect the efforts of the present rather than thinking that the last valid moment of Roman architecture was EUR and the Città Universitaria, which by the way is in great need of restoration. (S.B.)

Rome Centre

1. Richard Meier & Partners
Ara Pacis Museum
2. Francesco Cellini
Remodelling of the Mausoleo
di Augusto and Piazza Augusto
Imperatore
3. Juan Navarro Baldeweg
Bibliotheca Hertziana
4. Nemesi Studio
Museum Walkways
at the Mercati Traianei
5. Carlo Aymonino
Museum Space in the Campidoglio
6. ABDR
Reconstruction of the ex Serra
Piacentini at the Palazzo delle
Esposizioni
7. King Roselli Architetti
ES Hotel
8. 5+1AA
Remodelling of the ex Ferdinando
di Savoia Barracks
9. King Roselli Architetti
Pontificia Università Lateranense
Extension of the Pio IX Library

Rome Semicentre

10. The Office of Zaha Hadid
MAXXI – Museo nazionale
delle arti del XXI secolo
11. ABDR
Annibaliano B1 Metro Station
12. Odile Decq Benoît Cornette
Architectes Urbanistes
MACRO – Museo d'Arte
Contemporanea
13. ABDR
New Rome Tiburtina High
Speed Station
14. Labics
Città del Sole
15. Luciano Cupelloni
MACRO Future and Altra Economia
at the Mattatoio
16. Labics
Headquarters of Italpromo & Libardi
Associati
17. OMA – Office for Metropolitan
Architecture
Transformation of the Mercati
Generali

18. Giuseppe Pasquali,
Alfredo Passeri
Rectorate, Faculty and Department
of Law – Università Roma Tre
19. Sartogo Architetti Associati
Church of Sacro Volto di Gesù
20. n! studio
Storehouse-Laboratory
at Villa dei Quintili
21. Massimiliano Fuksas
Centro Congressi Italia at EUR

Rome Outskirts

22. Nemesi Studio
Church of Santa Maria
della Presentazione
23. Studio Valle Architetti Associati
Shopping Centre Porta di Roma
24. Francesco Cellini
and Andrea Salvioni
Secondary School
in Casal Monastero
25. Garofalo Miura
Church of Santa Maria Josefa
26. IaN+
Tor Vergata University Laboratories
27. Italo Rota & Associati
Church of Santa Margherita
Maria Alacoque
28. Architectuurstudio
Herman Hertzberger
School in Romanina
29. Marco Petreschi
Defence Administrative Centre
in Cecchignola
30. Monestiroli Architetti Associati
Church of San Carlo Borromeo
31. Umberto Riva
Church of San Guglielmo

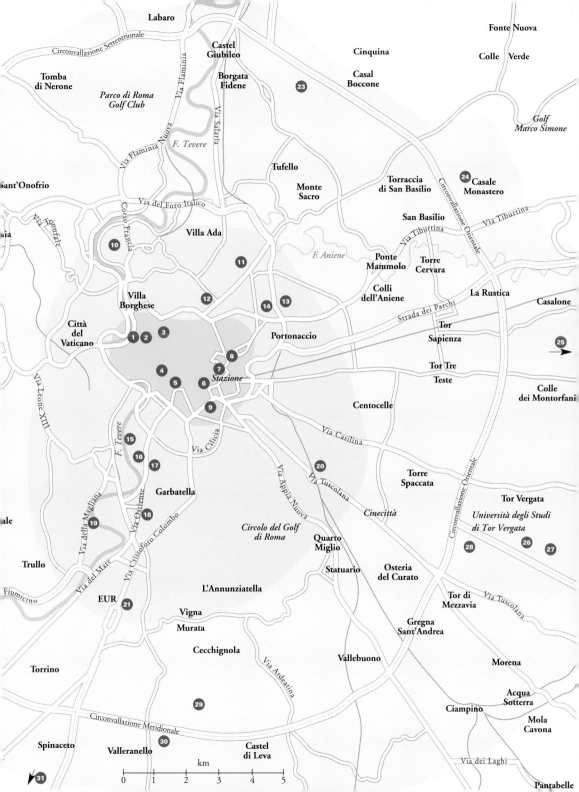

Contents

Schematic map of the main
circulation network
circumscribed by the Grande
Raccordo Anulare (GRA):
the Tiber and the Aniene rivers
are represented by dotted
lines; the three points indicate
the Capitol, the Stazione
Termini, and Piazza San Pietro.

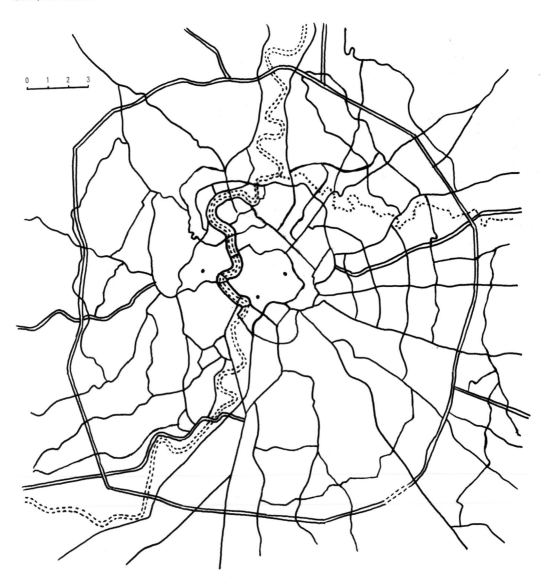

Rome_rome_ROME

Rome's image embraces a vast time span and draws on the current reality of the ancient. The Colosseum, Saint Peters, the Pantheon, Piazza Navona, the Trevi Fountain and the Trinità dei Monti are neither in an archaeological park nor in a museum. They are the heart of a city where people live, work and play. They are places where people have lived since time immemorial. In Rome the ancient is contemporary, an everyday event. The inauguration of the restored Palazzo delle Esposizioni (ABDR's project is among those presented in this book), with the Rothko exhibition, marked an important and sophisticated event for the city. However, when a would-be Neo-futurist reddened the waters of the Trevi Fountain two weeks later, the whole world was immediately abuzz about it. The icons of Rome embody the magic and aporia of this synchronism: the colour red like Anita Ekberg in the Trevi Fountain, Piazza San Pietro as Shibuya with the multitudes at the funeral of Pope John Paul II, the green fields in Piazza di Spagna in a famous biscuit commercial several years back. This does not mean that the city tends to suffocate the contemporary. On the contrary, it means—and as its icon show—that the image of Rome takes form precisely in the conflict between current happenings and the effects of history. It is as if catastrophe can never be the vehicle or the image of change in Rome; change in the Eternal City can only come about via anastylosis.

In other words, it would seem that the city already had a finished text that is continually reinterpreted in the readings of those who govern it, the tourism economy and popular culture. It is an open code that continually accepts being questioned but leaves little room for other writing. It can do without them. Renzo Piano had to drastically rework his plans for the Auditorium when they encountered the archaeological roots of the site. Zaha Hadid felt the need to anchor the fluid and flighty volumes of the MAXXI to one of the pavilions of the old barracks. In the Library of the Lateran University, King and Roselli recount the complexity and richness of a piece of architecture in Rome today using the language of the *Muro Torto*.

This secret and irrepressible soul of the city is always revealed in its finest works of architecture, from the most ancient to the most recent. The Colosseum is the monument that perhaps best helps us comprehend the relationship between Rome and its present. Its image appears fixed and immutable. It expresses an unmistakable identity. It is the archetype of classical antiquity. Yet, in taking a closer look, one finds that the Colosseum is crafted by a myriad of large and small changes, successive repairs or modifications, distortions of its sense. The brick buttress erected by Stern in 1807 to strengthen the monument shored up one end of the remaining outer ring and prevented its imminent collapse. The stone walls that compose the order of the façade were 'inscribed' upon the supporting buttress precisely at the moment when they were cracking and collapsing. It was an operation that seemed to make no concessions to the historical text, but its modern and functional nature becomes explicit precisely in its romantic conflict with the ruin. Less than thirty years later (1835), Giuseppe Valadier took the opposite approach in sealing and buttressing the other end of what remains of the outer wall, adhering to its essence and structural type. His buttress made of new bricks mimics the design and structure of the original walls, although he did not apply stone facework to it. In this case as well, the modernity of the project is openly declared. There was no desire to rediscover a lost meaning, but rather a desire to offer a new point of view on the nature of the monument. It matters little that the operations express opposing ideas about restoration work. What is interesting is how these two greatly differing and even conflicting approaches to describing and transforming the sense of the monument are present at the same time and in the same place and succeed in strengthening the character and identity of the Colosseum, adding other meanings and new imagery to the urban text.

What we now risk losing is precisely this type of fertile relation between the ancient soul of the city and the new which continually modifies and regenerates it. Or perhaps it is a question of conceiving this relation in a new and different manner.

At the beginning of an essay written several years ago (*Un'attualità perduta*, in *Topos e Progetto*, F.lli Palombi editori, Rome 2000), Franco Purini wrote: 'The figure of Giovan Battista Piranesi initiated the end of Rome. He marked the end of Rome as a central city for art and architecture, as a place capable of producing matchless exemplars, absolute paradigms, universal models projected into the future.'

Rome is among the Italian cities that have constructed the greatest number of buildings in the past ten years. In the four-year period 2004-2007, it increased its built volume by 80% (based on Cresme 2008 data for the province of Rome). This represents a new condition in terms of direct experience of place and changes in lifestyle, but not one that is manifested in the quality of the urban space or its architecture. The compact between the townspeople, building firms and political powers in Rome seems to exclude widespread quality. The new Master Plan Piano Regolatore Generale (PRG) calls for a massive growth of the city, but all the tension in the cultural debate focuses on the *genius loci* of the of the small building designed by Richard Meier to house the Ara Pacis, on the number and accessibility of services offered by Renzo Piano's Auditorium, the great cement walls of Hadid's museum, Fuksas' cloud, or the assignment to Santiago Calatrava for the Campus of the Seconda Università. As if a few architectural works out of the star system could or should compensate for the enormous weight of the new authorless city. But what damage will be wreaked upon Rome's urban environment, its countryside and its very image by the eighty million cubic metres of new construction spread out over time by the new Plan, or the seven million cubic metres built in 2007 and all those constructed previously?

While recorded in the statistics, this process of development of the built environment that is so profoundly changing the images and landscapes of the Eternal City is almost completely concealed in the media. The newly publicized image of Rome is not based on the quality of its urban growth, but on the technological development of businesses and the management capacity for large-scale events and massive tourist flows. The anastylosis drawing on the continual change that has always strengthened the image of the city as an architectural factory has now been interrupted. The urban icons of contemporary change are increasingly rare, weak and uncertain.

The enormous construction surge in Rome in recent years does not appear destined to leave many traces in the history of architecture. The rare works of value are often suffocated and lost among the exuberant projects of the star system and the impetus of the construction and real estate economy.

With the patience of a diviner, Sebastiano Brandolini accompanies us on the discovery of new quality architecture among the onrush of cubic metre after cubic metre that is submerging the city. His research maps out an interesting and unexpected itinerary that allows us to discern the cultural dimension of the ongoing construction processes and gain new perspectives on today's Rome.

Brandolini's volume makes no apologies in describing the new architectures of Rome. It clearly identifies the new metropolitan reality of Rome as a central and latent figure, something that has yet to be realized. It identifies the main players in the changes and highlights the objectives and impacts of their policies on the city. In short, if one reads it as the tale of a city under stress, then other figures and factors—beyond the architecture and the city itself—emerge as protagonists to affirm the virtues of the approach taken in the book, helping the reader reconstruct the contexts that seem to vanish as the city advances.

Here—as we read between the lines—the three great patrons of change, each with their own urban strategy, play a decisive role. The Public Administration (applied to which, the word 'caste' is gaining increasing currency in Italy) increasingly appropriates the most prestigious historical settings for itself and seeks to attach its name to high visibility projects for a few new public buildings (museums, transportation nodes, convention centres, etc.), leaving to Rome the small monuments of a distracted era. The Church has systematically and quite successfully demonstrated (at least since the fifteenth century) that it knows how to propose praiseworthy architecture—perhaps the best recent works in Rome—as expressions of an accumulated urban culture and nodes of social aggregation in the more marginal areas. And lastly, private builders are the principal players in the building boom without qualities, in the multitude of new houses that invade the territory without possessing sufficient attributes to merit inclusion in studies such as this one on noteworthy works of built architecture.

On the other hand, the book fails to present a single park, or a project addressing the existing context, or a piece of architecture that expresses a position of some significance regarding environmental issues. This is not a question of omissions or censorship; the book presents a truthful snapshot of a Rome that is still incapable of responding to the great themes, ranging from habitat quality to sustainable development, associated with the metropolis in the third millennium.

But the strength of the book lies in containing both a tale and a vision. Among the presented works, the most interesting are those that are still little known and interpret the new urban condition 'with a certain detachment' (5+1AA, King Roselli, Navarro Baldeweg) and those scattered along the ring of the Grande Raccordo Anulare (Greater Ring Road) 'where new identities and the future gravitate' (Clemente e Molè, Garofalo, IaN+, Petreschi, Rota). These completed projects express the propositional and visionary soul of the book. Its originality lies in the way it manages to describe, with a taxonomy of recent quality architectural works, the potential forebears of a new urban geography.

It is a description that projects the new image of Rome onto an enlarged landscape, as in the film by Virzì, with *its whole life ahead*. Its fluid centre is on the Raccordo Anulare, on the huge flowing magnet of a metropolitan organization that still awaits invention, where the new architecture recounted by the book tends to collect. They are the spaces that best interpret the transformations at the start of the millennium, those that demonstrate that there is another possibly viable idea of Rome. They are spaces, in other words, that seek to implement the paradigm of the Colosseum in different architectural languages, giving sense to change and new imageries to the city.

Renzo Piano Building Workshop,
Auditorium; top right,
the Flaminio Stadium.

The Tor Sapienza industrial
zone along Via Prenestina,
2000

Sebastiano Brandolini   # State and Church

Where is Rome's relationship with contemporary architecture? Are they on the same wavelength? The Master Plan – Piano Regolatore Generale, by Giuseppe Campos Venuti and approved in March 2006, plans for strong growth in the city's metropolitan dimensions. In the meantime there has been a succession of competitions, bidding contests and expectations regarding both the small and the large scale, all duly publicized. The former mayors Francesco Rutelli (1993-2001) and Walter Veltroni (2001-2008) both invested municipal resources and staked their credibility on the belief that Rome—the eternal city and Italy's most populous—is capable of generating a modern image for itself and competing in the urban marketing arena with other European capital cities. Paris, London, Berlin, Barcelona, and others have made architecture one of their standard-bearers and rely on its power of attraction. This is Rome's most recent attempt to overturn with concrete deeds the weighty urban-planning legacy of its post-war period; Rome has long been behind in its engagement with the present. The standard text on this topic remains Italo Insolera's *Roma moderna. Un secolo di storia urbanistica 1870-1970*, with the most recent edition published in 2001. Perhaps we will find more recent years addressed in the next edition.

For these reasons and others, this volume conducts an analysis of the field, sketching a portrait of the buildings of contemporary Rome. If you have a few days to spend, and you do not want to dedicate them to ancient, early-Christian, Byzantine, Renaissance, Baroque or Fascist Rome, what should you see to get an idea of today's architecture in Rome? Where will you find works that will leave you with a sense of beauty, research and discovery that refer to the present? In spite of the city's increasing interest in its contemporary look, it is not easy to find full-fledged works that fully reward our senses. This must be due to the inexplicably long periods that always seem to separate conception from realization, or to the enervating bureaucratic stratification that thickens and slows the flow of any procedure or idea, or perhaps to the absence of any collective goal. But more than matters of culpability, these objective problems seem to be mutual causes of a malaise that makes itself felt almost everywhere in Italy, but that becomes particularly visible in Rome. We still need to understand really why contemporary architecture in Rome more often than not appears out of place. The instinctual question arises: *cui prodest* (who benefits from) contemporary architecture? Few are the works realized in Rome in recent years where one clearly recognizes the timbre of ineffable simplicity and quality that has been modern architecture's inspiration for nearly a century and in which Europe, the old continent, is especially well endowed.

Aerial view of illegal developments around Rome, c. 1975.

What makes Rome unique among the large European cities that have witnessed strong growth this past century is its quality of appearing uninterrupted. Its physical aspect (which makes it strangely similar to Berlin) has been the subject of disquisitions by, among others, such disparate architects as Paolo Portoghesi and Franco Purini, who have found a dialectical meaning in interruption on which to base their urbanistic theories. It is interesting, but perhaps not surprising, to observe how Giovanni Battista Piranesi's fantastic layout of Campo Marzio of 1762 resembles the scheme of a host of suburbs designed in the 1970s and 1980s. In Rome, a city that has virtually all but abandoned the quest for an overall transportation policy (because, it is said, the subsurface is impracticable), identity and archaeology constitute an indissoluble dyad, while archaeology constitutes the genetic code of interruption, which has continued its self-nurtured growth over the years.

In *Roma moderna*, Italo Insolera states that, by deciding not to tear down the Aurelian Walls when it became Italy's capital in 1871, Rome denied itself a potential identity as a modern city, resolving not to bring past and present, inside and outside, into a single vision. Today we sense that Rome is repeating the same error on the metropolitan scale, finding it difficult to come to terms with its true dimensions and not admitting that its future can only depend on a vision that includes development of infrastructure and transportation. The totality of transportation can and must prevail over the particularity of the new centralities underway. The meaning and success of much architecture in recent and in future years has depended and will continue to depend on its placement within a general scheme, and on its capacity to share and be part of clearly defined urban planning goals. Green areas, parking facilities, new districts, rivers, shopping centres, and the Grande Raccordo Anulare should all contribute to creating a harmonious framework, and within it, accompany the city on its process of incessant metropolitan transformation. In Rome, as in many other Italian cities, urban planning seems to be more a survey of the *status quo* than a project; more than being a future prospect, it is an excrescence of the present. If Rome's twenty-two Nuove Centralità, disconnected from one another in terms of the transportation network, satisfy the city's numerical growth forecast for the upcoming decades, they nevertheless exclude the road and rail transport network from their individual identities. The transport network should be ascribed the role of nervous system rather than merely a circulatory system.

Having abandoned the vision that matured in the 1970s and that was condensed into the functional axes of the Sistema Direzionale Orientale (SDO), Rome now seems to pursue fragmentary projects that are subsequently and summarily stitched back together, none of which has sufficient specific weight to shift any equilibria. Streets, housing and green areas, physical things capable of acting as connective tissue on which to build the whole city, do not appear to be of much interest to the public administration, the community of architects, or to the construction firms. Worse yet, when a way is found to make the interests of these three categories coincide, the results more often than not wreak havoc on quality control. The image that Rome gives itself today (*Roma oggi* is the title of a 1977 book by Leonardo Benevolo) is that of a city composed principally of monuments or landmarks, each of which is a beacon in competition with the others. Paradoxically, archaeology, which is often presented as a guarantee of continuity and long duration for the city, appears to be partially responsible for the spatial-temporal syncopes characterizing the city fabric.

The best recent architectural works in Rome are those that are simple, modest and devoid of any rhetoric. They are works that assume an almost imperceptible appearance of calm and unassuming modernity. Declining to make grand gestures, conceived with careful attention to detail, practical and direct, some have already been built, others are being built and still others are still on paper. They have nothing to do with the usual idea of Rome impressed upon our minds, a vision associated with postcards, antiquity, monuments and grand gestures. Perhaps there is meaning to be found in the fact that their architects are not Roman, and so they see and find in Rome things that those who have the city before their eyes every day cannot see or sense. Among these architects we have Juan Navarro Baldeweg from Spain (who worked on the extension of the Bibliotheca Hertziana), King and Roselli (King is from London, Roselli from Rome, they built a hotel next to Termini station and an excellent library at the Lateran University), Umberto Riva and Italo Rota from Milan (each of whom has a Roman church to his credit), and Pietro Valle's studio out of Friuli (creator of a major shopping centre in the northern part of the city). The sensation is that in order to work well, instead of knowledge of the tribulations and planning perversions of the city, what Rome needs is a certain detachment from itself. Rather than memory, what it needs is a sort of culturally endowed psychological repression, a sense of responsibility and farsightedness.

There are many public projects and buildings: museums, transportation facilities, churches, schools and offices. In Rome, architecture principally represents the public sector (state, city, church) rather than the private sector (and this is a clear and important difference with respect to Milan). What strikes the eye in Rome, apart from the dramatic absence of quality housing, is the almost total non-existence of quality hotels and office buildings, architectural types which otherwise are certainly not lacking. Offices and housing are considered ordinary architecture and construction work, market segments that have little or nothing in common with the noble aspirations of churches and museums. The city pays, and will continue to pay, a high price for this mental forgetfulness. The greater the scale and complexity of Greater Rome, the more short-sighted its projects seem to be.

Rome is not the only Italian city whose identity and future gravitate increasingly upon the ring road that encircles it, creating a rather well-defined boundary. We see the same thing in Turin, Milan, Bologna, Venice-Mestre and Naples. Their *tangenziali*, initially developed as connections between the motorways feeding the city, over the years have attracted mass market functions that the city centres saw as undesirable. Subsequently, in becoming linear cities with an almost exclusively commercial vocation, they have become bona fide pieces of the city, without however obtaining the rightful recognition and attention. The sublevel placement of the Grande Raccordo Anulare (GRA) under the Parco dell'Appia Antica sends an important signal regarding the relationship Rome is seeking to institute between the city and

its infrastructure and the surrounding countryside. The GRA (object of an interesting study by Mario De Quarto) is approximately 70 kilometres long, but it continues to be perceived as the 'rear end' of the true city; perhaps we have reached the moment to see it as a front, not only in terms of publicity, but also in terms of meaning.

We also note a prejudice—comprising expectations, controls, quality and decreasing results—between what is done in the centre, in the surrounding ring, and in the outskirts of Rome. This prejudice is understandable but not admissible, because the environment is certainly no less important in those places where it is more vulnerable or degraded. Perhaps we should state the contrary, given that there is more need of quality in places where there is less of it. And so it is at least as surprising, when it happens, to find quality far from the centre as it is to find mediocrity in the centre. It is important that the city not be dismembered on the basis of contrasting expectations, while the hierarchy of quality cannot be determined just by conservational prescriptions and restrictive decalogues. We must not be deceived by the metropolitan legend that the Roman suburbs—thanks to the cinematography of Vittorio De Sica (*Bicycle Thieves*, 1948), Roberto Rossellini (*Roma città aperta*, 1945), Pier Paolo Pasolini (*Mamma Roma*, 1962) and Nanni Moretti (*Caro diario*, 1993)—have earned the distinction of *genius loci*. Still today, all you have to do is visit two new churches built toward the outlying hills, one by Garofalo Miura and the other by Italo Rota, to remind yourself that in the final analysis the city is composed of qualitative and quantitative standards and that architecture in substance is a service. In the deep desolation of the districts where these two beautiful churches stand, stores are missing, there are few streets and the only readable rule is that of exploiting the land. If the churches are bridgeheads with architectural, social, urbanistic and symbolic responsibilities, then the priests are explorers of a virgin territory that must be surveyed, ploughed, and made fertile. And the schools and teachers that populate these areas have a similar importance and role. Under the warehouse-like church designed by Rota in Tor Vergata, we sense the fragrance of something heroic that claws at our chests and makes us wonder: why does life in the outskirts have to be so harsh and pitiable? Can architecture on its own sustain the weight and dreams for a quality living environment?

Berlin, Barcelona, Paris, London and also many smaller cities now include contemporary architectural works among their tourist attractions, something which helps finance the general municipal budget. If the same will happen in the future in Rome, it will mean that contemporary architecture and art have joined forces with the ancient, Renaissance and Baroque art of which Rome is overflowing. But in Rome, those who claim to believe in the liberating beauty of contemporary architecture only half believe. They have reservations and emphasize the 'buts.' Contemporary architecture—of whatever making—has always met with conditions of mental guardedness. This is perceived by those who visit the space that might have been the showpiece of contemporary Roman architecture: the roof of the Giardino Romano behind the Palazzo dei Conservatori, at the Campidoglio. What better place to craft a jewel that would have awakened the city from the torpor of the past fifty years? But Carlo Aymonino did not dedicate sufficient attention to accomplishing such a delicate programme, which involved the display of the original equestrian statue of Marcus Aurelius, other archaeological relics, and an enormous piece of the wall of the temple of Jupiter Capitolinus discovered during excavation work. The twelve long years that passed between the decision to proceed and the inauguration of the space were certainly useful in carrying out the necessary philological analyses and obtaining all the necessary administrative permits, but not for producing a convincing work of architecture. The demanding cosmopolitan tourist, who comes to admire at close range the large bronze sculpture that was moved here to protect it from atmospheric pollutants, will only feel disappointment at the ramshackle and summary setting that frames it. This micro-architecture by Aymonino, a meritorious urban theoretician in the 1960s and 1970s and Assessore al Centro Storico from 1981 to 1985, could have represented a courageous testament. Unfortunately his work is just a disappointment devoid of all character and form, and composed of dime-a-dozen materials and fixtures.

Richard Meier's Ara Pacis Museum, strongly supported by Francesco Rutelli during his mayorship, stirred up a lively debate and is today under threat by the couple composed by Gianni Alemanno and Vittorio Sgarbi. It is a coherent work, in line with Meier's conviction that the formal rhetoric of the Corbusian pavilion is still a must: a ductile, solar, universal language. Meier, in touching on the classic themes of modern architecture (glass, podium, circulation, light), collided with the cultural, political and formal intrigue of Rome in these years. Rome, in fact, is going through a revisionist phase regarding the architecture from the twenty years of Fascism and experiencing the certainty that it seems to offer. Piazza Augusto Imperatore (object of competition won by Francesco Cellini's group) is one of the stages. Many asked: 'What has Meier got to do with this piazza?' Local citizens and architects emphasized that the New York architect's style was foreign to those parts: his blindingly white plasterboard walls appear shrill against their megalithic travertine neighbours, its neo-purist lightness clashes with the monumental stereometry of the porticoes designed by Vittorio Ballio Morpurgo in 1938. In short, the city's first concern is contextual harmony, a legacy that sooner or later will have to be outgrown.

To the stylistic doubts raised by Ara Pacis however, we have to add that it is a building created with great care and without cutting corners, every part of it painstakingly conceived and designed, with details and materials that are the fruit of a thinking and development process pursued with total professionality. And it is also a success with visitors. Few other Roman buildings can make the same claim. In too many of them we read the signs of irregular worksite management characterized by conflict and half measures. Architecture is like a fossil: once it is built it tells no lies, revealing all. The pitiless eye reads all its defects and discerns blame.

Another building running counter-current to the prevalent praxis and demonstrating that it is possible to react against approximation and interpret beauty through precision stands behind the Basilica of San Giovanni in Laterano. It is the Library of the Lateran University by King Roselli, who also designed the Es Hotel between Via Giolitti and Via Turati, next to the tracks

Following pages: the Grande Raccordo Anulare at the tunnel under the Parco dell'Appia Antica.

of Termini station. The library is a special place. Its interior is composed of two vertically juxtaposed parallelepipeds that share an internal face. One parallelepiped is a packet of six floors stuffed with books like a large open-sided bookcase; the other is a full-height space crossed by three gentle ramps, each one connecting two levels and sufficiently wide to accommodate the reading desks. The void space of the reading room, hovering in the air, produces a strong atmosphere of collegiality. Natural light descends from deep slanting window-slashes in the façades. From the interior, the ramps create a curious interplay of counterposed inclined planes. From the outside, the same windows play counterpoint to the composure of the ecclesiastic façades of the surrounding buildings.

There is another library, still under construction, that is destined to become one of the finest buildings of these years: the Bibliotheca Hertziana. The client is the Max-Planck Institute. The architect is the Spaniard Juan Navarro Baldeweg. This legendary institute organized an invited competition in 1995. Participants included Carlo Aymonino and Vittorio De Feo. Baldeweg's winning design is delicate and graceful, a wood and metal frame lowered from above between the sixteenth-century Palazzo Zuccari and the nineteenth-century Palazzo Stroganoff, cutting out a tiny internal courtyard reminiscent of a cloister. Thus the traces of the urban theatre are proposed anew, as happened on the same spot in Roman times (just above today's Piazza di Spagna there once stood a Roman villa) and later in the Baroque period. Baldeweg dealt with the archaeology by stitching in a refined architectonic patch that emphasizes the site's deep vertical section, typical of the adjacent buildings above Via Gregoriana.

A city of Rome's dimensions cannot pacify its relationship with contemporary architecture merely via individual works, but is obliged to address the theme of collective planning. Three emblematic projects were launched in the 1990s: the Parco della Musica (Renzo Piano, 2002); the church in Tor Tre Teste (Richard Meier, 2001) and the functional upgrade of Termini station (2001). The first addresses entertainment, the second spirituality and the third transportation. None of them addressed the theme of history, often perceived as being emblematic of Rome's identity as a city turned toward its past. The three buildings inaugurated a new vantage point on the city with respect to its architectural present, which after so many years no longer arouses fear. There followed waves of design contests addressing themes relating to loci for socialization that people and communities could identify with. There were competitions for piazzas, churches and schools. This proliferation of small competitions demanded—in addition to a noteworthy bureaucratic and administrative effort—faith and optimism. But in the tentacular metropolis (the consular roads remain the main axes of growth) these contests were mere drops in an ocean. Small scale, mono-functional and incapable of serving as spearheads for anything, piazzas, churches and schools described on a miniature scale precisely those aspirations for community that is often felt to be lacking.

Like pioneering plant species that take root in virgin soil and make it inhabitable, the churches act as forward outposts for the rapid real-estate occupation of the *Agro Romano* (Roman countryside), which many feel has already vanished. Even when their placement appeared improbable, it only enhanced their almost surreal charm and allure. Their sacredness is recognized by the small symbols that stand out. In contexts lacking in any planning, churches are often the only places where order and intentionality can be recognized. This gives them something in common with true civic settings. The Church of Santa Margherita Maria Alacocque, designed by Italo Rota and built on the spot where Pope John Paul II celebrated the grand Jubilee mass in Tor Vergata, deliberately implements this curious regression, returning to the status of a house. It is a boxy structure reduced to a minimum of signs, as a child would have drawn it, faced in sky-blue cladding and adorned with a red cross just above the entrance. The adjacent bell tower is a sort of caricature that deforms the geometry of the church as it rises, transforming into a pylon. Optimistic, this pop-style church makes a meaningful contribution to the academic spirit that hovers in the air of Tor Vergata, and presages that even this disjointed, inconclusive edge city will one fine day be attributed its own *genius loci*.

There is a fatalistic conviction among various architects that, Rome being an improvised assemblage of different interpretations of modernity, this is the only course that can be pursued, in that it is a characteristic trait of Rome's identity. It is certainly a different Romanity than the pompous one trumpeted by the Fascists or the realist one of the post-war years. This is an empirical Romanity, suburban and opportunist. The eclectic church designed by Pietro Sartogo is a good example of this. Here the Roman style is carefully crafted to the point that it composes a complete mythology of the village: the running balcony with a decorative wrought iron railing, the oculus reminiscent of Baroque trompe-l'œil, the internal passageways that bring to life a picturesque microcosm, the many viewpoints, collaborations with artists, and the fragmentation of the religious imagery. Overall, a vision is preached of the church as a dramatic *via crucis*, rather than a static place of peace and quiet. Sartogo's curious church dazzles the eye with its polysemous linguistic references.

A feeling of exuberance is also transmitted by the hyper-three-dimensionality of the church in Quartaccio, the work of Nemesi Studio, which blends religious and civic characters and is made of cold, lightweight materials that can hardly be expected to withstand the severe tests of time and use. Here the religious aspect is expressed by platonic forms hanging in midair, while the civic element is condensed into the eloquent and articulated portico area, which acts as a liaison between the different ecclesiastic functions, the residential district and the sports centre behind the church. The church, rich in metallic grey tones and interplays of half-shadows, is a deconstructed architectonic object, perhaps too smart and fine for the harsh Pasolinian reality that fifty years after the publication of *Ragazzi di vita* is still the sensation and life experience in Quartaccio. To cope with this problem, the church has been transformed from an open piazza to an enclosed refuge, much to the detriment of its intended meaning and utility.

Perhaps, rather than dedicating itself to the exceptionality of some places, Rome should direct its attention to the common man. Adolf Loos said as much one century ago, hoping to resolve everyone's problems by way of simplicity.

Following pages: aerial view of the crowd of 'pope-boys' and the papal stage (by the architect Marco Petreschi) built in Tor Vergata for the 15th World Youth Day, Grand Jubilee of 2000.

But it would seem that the common man today does not ask for the help of an architect or a technician to resolve his practical problems; he is convinced that he can resolve them on his own. He asks the architect to give birth to fantastic images endowed with auras and unrepeatability, one-of-a-kind buildings. Rather than parking facilities, new infrastructure networks or energy savings, he wants spectacles, impressive displays that are inspired by the imagery disgorged daily from his televisions, the ubiquitous jack-in-the-box. The common Italians, incapable of distinguishing between parliamentary and televised debates, think that they need projects that can compete with the lofty monuments that constitute the landmarks of the eternal city: cupolas, prospects, bold lines, media effects. In *Learning from Las Vegas* (1972), Robert Venturi hypothesized—half-seriously—a parentage between Rome and the Nevada city: illusory worlds on which to project images, desires and dreams. In *Roma*, Federico Fellini equates Rome with Cinecittà.

There are two projects, one still on paper and the other at an advanced stage of construction, that, thanks to seductive computer renderings and the overwhelming power of the media, might influence the future mythology of Rome, like the EUR district did some seventy years ago. Their architects reassure us saying that, yes, they are two innovative buildings, but nevertheless rooted in necessity. The first is Massimiliano Fuksas' Convention Centre in the EUR, and the second is Zaha Hadid's MAXXI in Flaminio. The fifteen or so kilometres separating them may suffice to redefine the cultural geography of the city centre, elongating it along a north-south axis. Offspring of the entertainment culture, these projects aspire to become icons of the near future, architectural pilgrimage sites. The Convention Centre has grounded its fame on a container-cloud dichotomy, two immaterial forms; Fuksas equates the former to banality, the latter to reverie. For bureaucratic and financial reasons, Fuksas so far has had trouble realizing his dream, but it now appears that the project is moving forward. Some ten years have passed since he won the competition. These practical problems were compounded by issues of an artistic nature: how to actually build the intangible structure of the cloud so that it expresses the vaporous lightness desired by the architect at all hours of the day?

The images of the MAXXI distributed by Hadid's studio are mainly bird's-eye views. The project concept is to discover latent itineraries in the surrounding context and make the architectural work a truly integral and integrating component of the city. It is not meant to be a fortified, forbidding area, but one that allows people to cross through it and move within it freely. The images provided by the Anglo-Iraqi artist-architect draw us into hyper-dynamics and expectations that are not likely to be perceived from the much more earthly reality of the streets, entrances and halls. The Padiglione Italia at the 2006 Venice Biennale exhibited photographs of the MAXXI construction site by a variety of different photographers commissioned by the Direzione Generale per l'Architettura e l'Arte Contemporanee (DARC); these images amplified the sense of expectation that envelopes the real substance of the MAXXI's sinuous curves. In any case, if the MAXXI wins the same public acclaim enjoyed by Piano's nearby Parco della Musica, a new cultural hub will have been established north of the city centre.

The iconicity pursued by the buildings of Fuksas and Hadid collides with the crude reality of the city, without necessarily alleviating it. A city's quality level is the result of the mean of all its pieces; it is not determined by the height of its peaks. A large former industrial area along Via Ostiense is the object of a redevelopment project that also encompasses the shores along the Tiber and the nearby Testaccio district. The Public Administration's intention is to see this area become a part of the city dedicated to young people, to education, informal culture and alternative markets. Via Ostiense starts at the Aurelian Walls not far from the large green field of the Circus Maximus, and ends, just over a mile away (the same length as Via del Corso), in the green area surrounding the Basilica of San Paolo fuori le mura. Some years ago in this area, Francesco Cellini designed roofs to protect excavations, bringing nature and archaeology together under the same frame. Today, the state of abandonment and disrepair of these small works is painful to behold and spurs thought on the form that the synergy between modernity and archaeology might assume in the future.

There is a whole series of projects along Via Ostiense. The transformation of the Centrale Montemartini into a museum (by Francesco Stefanori) is a successful example. Le Corbusier had intuited the possible complicity between the stonework of classical antiquity and the pure and functional forms of the metallic industrial machine. The decoration and atmosphere stimulate the visitors, making them re-experience works that we might otherwise have had to consider dead and gone. The same certainly cannot be said of the mediocre museum space at the Chiostro Michelangiolesco (next to the Church of Santa Maria degli Angeli) in the Baths of Diocletian (by Giovanni Bulian). Across Via Ostiense from the Centrale Montemartini stands one of the most intelligent buildings constructed in Rome in recent years, where the values of normality and tranquillity are combined. It is the Faculty of Law designed by Giuseppe Pasquali and Alfredo Passeri on the swath of land along the rail line. They chose brick as their material and the simple and direct parallelepiped, cylinder and cube as their forms. They are arranged in such a way as to facilitate the use of the open spaces as pathways, passages, and places to stop a bit, and to expand the already great width of Via Ostiense. In a city as big as Rome, there should be many civic and civil architectural works such as this. The Faculty of Law could function as a prototype for sparking a collective debate on the language and construction of the city.

The nearby Mattatoio is a *castrum* (military camp) covering approximately a dozen hectares where you may intuit, better than in other zones such as Tor Vergata or Flaminio, Rome's desire to moult and renew itself. Its broad open spaces prefigure new perceptions, functions and lifestyles; it is very important in Rome to insert new and well-dosed urban functions. The Mattatoio, as its name states, was historically a logistics centre for livestock slaughter. Its buildings arranged in rows have the discrete and universal charm of archetypes that we often look for in architecture. It was this quality that prevented their demolition in the thirty years since their abandonment. Now, various public entities have reached a good-neighbour agreement; the leitmotif of the project is reuse. The two beautiful buildings composing

Santiago Calatrava, Sport City
in Tor Vergata, model of project.

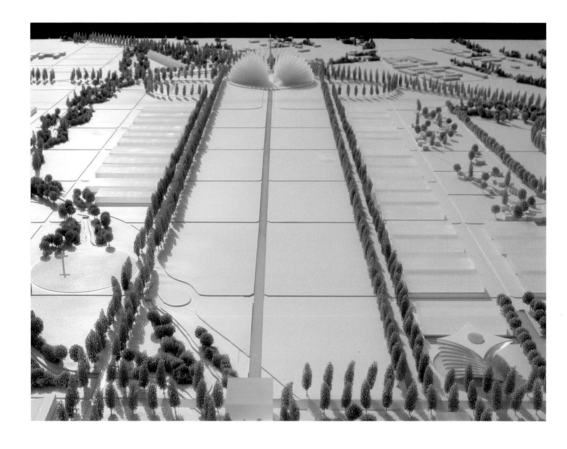

Gregotti Associati International,
the new Acilia district, model
of project.

the façade on Piazza Orazio Giustiniani have been redeveloped as arts venues with all the necessary technical systems. Some portions were replaced and mezzanine floors were installed. Their internal façades give onto a large courtyard where other activities and functions take place. In the other large courtyard just to the south, another redeveloped linear building will accommodate an alternative, non-profit market. Although the overall quality of the facilities leaves something to be desired, the project intermixes old and new fragments and materials within a generally high quality design, whose meaning however leans more strongly to the political and urbanistic rather than to the architectural. In the attempt to get beyond a viewpoint of pure conservation, the Mattatoio prefigures a possible strategy for reusing former industrial spaces, a strategy that can neither be improvised nor left to its own devices.

The feeling is that the Roman superintendencies are slowly coming to the realization that conservation is a means, not an end. The end has to be the achievement of quality in urban design and the creation of a virtuous circle that does not automatically exclude contemporary inputs. The system of walkways created at the Mercati Traianei by Nemesi Studio, an emblematic case for all to see, could be used as a conceptual matrix for the recovery and enhancement of other archaeological ruins.

The project by ABDR for the Palazzo delle Esposizioni on Via Nazionale calls into question the perception of a pompous building, seeking sources of redemption among the various parts added after its original construction. Among these we have the interesting skylights from the 1980s by Costantino Dardi, which quite rightly were recovered. The Serra Piacentini takes new form and becomes a floating glass pavilion creating a dual visual connection: outside towards the raised area of the gardens along Via del Quirinale, and inside toward the new entrance on the street level. The difficult mission of the new pavilion is the reconciliation of different stylistic moments.

5+1AA approaches the redevelopment theme inflicting a more 'violent' deviation from the original building and seeking a complete upending of meaning. Their first proving grounds in Rome is a building typical of the gigantism that was in vogue one hundred years ago, the Castro Pretorio, future home for offices of the Interior Ministry. The salient points of their renovation project are the vertical stair connections and the roof. Cement stairs, reminiscent of Luigi Moretti, pursue expressive forms as they move in the void freed up by corner floor demolitions. The roof, redesigned in a French mode, enhances the use of interior surfaces; viewed from Termini station, it is unfortunately a very dissonant element in the delicate Roman skyline.

It is not easy for any city to give a coherent response regarding what cultural camp it belongs to, but oftentimes urban planning and architecture help project a shared horizon. Rome is pursuing a strategy, regarding both quantity and quality, that might be termed 'piecemeal.' Before its grandness—which it bears rather than plans—Rome takes refuge in small things, in a fragmented management of its urban heritage. The urbanistic theorem on which Rome seems to ground its bets for the future is this: in the age of scepticism, fragmentation of power and of responsibility, distrust in the public sector, the parcelling out of land, and absence of systems, urban democracy and justice themselves become subjective, indeterminate and aleatory. The feeling is that, in order to create broad consensus, Rome continues to refuse a clear idea of architecture: museums and shopping centres, a few new buildings in the centre, expansion zones, local improvements in infrastructure, symbols scattered here and there, and a few piazzas, schools and churches and a bit of lotting. Talking about Rome's extraordinary and eternal beauty, as people so often end up doing, is certainly no help in resolving the city's functional problems. Instead, it casts a discouraging veil of ineluctability over any possible improvement on an adequate scale.

In its convulsive demographic growth after the long post-war period, Rome still affirms its identity today as a city composed of dwellings. Yet, in a classic act of psychological repression, this theme is completely lacking from the issues that the city currently addresses. The sporadic attempts at investigating the theme, such as the study conducted by the Osservatorio Nomade on the Corviale housing block (original design by Mario Fiorentino, 1973-1981), appear isolated and have no outcomes on the community level. Even though the study of the Corviale found a real outlet, as things stand there is no sign of either the will or the ability to get to work on such intricate political problems. Corviale was born deformed and never witnessed the construction of the many neighbouring buildings that were originally planned. But with respect to many nearby buildings put up today, it possesses an enviably visionary stature. In today's Europe, many cities have based their urban planning policy on the theme of housing, and the ancillary effects on green areas, mobility, density and functional mix. The large Bijlmer district, developed in the 1960s southeast of Amsterdam, largely demolished and redesigned over the last decade, might serve as a reference point to free and open thinking on the issue of housing.

Giovanni Battista Piranesi, *Ruins of mausoleums along Via Appia*, (from Antichità Romane, Vol. III, 1756).

Rome Centre

1

Ara Pacis Museum

Richard Meier
& Partners

The Ara Pacis Museum is designed to house the ancient Ara Pacis Augustae, a sacrificial altar dating to 9 b.C. The museum is an integral part of the urban context of the Augustan area of Rome. The altar was originally housed in a building designed by Vittorio Ballio Morpurgo in 1938. The new architectural design protects the relic located along the Tiber, near the Ponte Cavour, on the western edge of the Piazza Augusto Imperatore.

The Ara Pacis Museum is the first work of modern architecture in the historic center of Rome since the 1930s. The clarity of the volumes and the building's proportions relate in scale to Rome's ancient structures. One predominating feature of the new building is a glass curtain wall, 13.5 meters high and 50 meters long. The asymmetrical 8.5-meter-high entry hall, defined by seven slender columns in reinforced concrete finished with white waxed marble plaster, leads to the main hall, which houses the Ara Pacis.

The contrast between the subdued lighting of the entrance space and the expansive top-lit and rigorously symmetrical Great Hall encourages a naturally progressive circulation. The roof over the Great Hall rests on four columns with skylights to ensure the most natural lighting and to eliminate 'false shadows.'

Outside the main structure, a low travertine wall extending from within the Great Hall traces the ancient shore of the Tiber. Building materials include glass and concrete and an indigenous fine beige Roman travertine.

The building provides 700 square meters of space for temporary exhibitions and installations dedicated to archaeological themes and includes a state-of-the-art digital library of Augustan culture. An outdoor roof terrace above the auditorium is an essential part of the circulation. It includes a contiguous bar and café with views over the Mausoleo di Augusto to the east and the Tiber to the west.

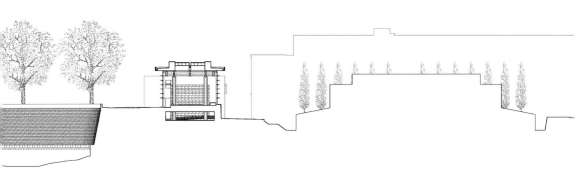

Previous pages: cross section
and views from the south.
Right: the interior with the Ara
Pacis. Following pages: view
with the Church
of San Rocco and with
the Mausoleo di Augusto,
and ground floor plan.

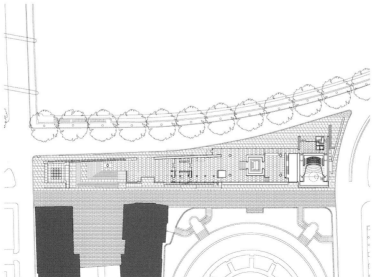

2

Remodelling of the Mausoleo di Augusto and Piazza Augusto Imperatore

Francesco Cellini

We are in the centre of Rome, between the Tiber and Via del Corso, between the oldest aquatic artery that connects the city to the sea and the historical urban axis extending northwards from the Campidoglio. The great Augustan landmark characterizing the site, immobile for two millennia but continually assailed by and physically involved in urban development, stands at the centre of gravity signifying its proper historicity.

The project must address issues on two levels: at the geometrical centre of the complex, there is uncertainty regarding the original placement of the emperor's tomb, a 'black hole' at the centre of a gravitational field; in the urban surroundings, the painful, disquieting decompression caused by the radical demolitions of the 1930s.

Today, the goal is to reject the rigid isolation of the Augustan Mausoleum and re-establish its role as a protagonist. Its new prominent image will be achieved via an iconic separation taking the form of a broad, uncluttered, green parterre and a volumetric uplifting taking the form of a lofty crown of holm oaks. This new architectural setting for the monument will place it in visual and spatial relation with its urban setting without requiring new load bearing structures.

Two different situations are thus configured: a central void and a surrounding network of interrelations. The void evokes an ancient sacredness awaiting answers. The sense of sonority in the cylindrical void pervaded by a sense of sacredness and the role of the ancient and mysterious labyrinthine plan will be evoked by the effects and the reversibility of *ars topiaria* (ornamental gardening).

In the surrounding context, the 'archaeological' isolation will be replaced by a revitalization of urban interconnections drawing power from the sense of expectation aroused by the monument. A loose network of interrelations is thus generated with its closest monumental nodes in the three churches and the Ara Pacis Museum, and others to be found in nearby landmarks of the Tiber and Via del Corso. On the urban scale this network will reach its finer branches to historical landmarks, topologically more distant but intensely interrelated: the Pantheon and Castel Sant'Angelo first and foremost, and also the Campidoglio, the Gianicolo and the Pincio.

The primary monumental interlocution, generated from the spatial connections created by the new urban design, is grounded in a dialectic between greenery and stone, and is configured along broad contextual reconnections. The most demanding external work is a vast system of tiers that evokes an image of urban theatre which has now disappeared but is still present in the collective historical memory (the eighteenth-century Scalinata di Ripetta) and also evokes a function that has been rooted in this place for centuries: public entertainment. The work on the urban fabric starts with the elimination of the unsightly depression that surrounds the Augustan Mausoleum, marred by pretentious stairways and an unkempt garden. The depression will be filled with soil, creating a piazza-garden by means of a simple raising of the ground level so as not to jeopardize any new archaeological investigations. The project thus links to the memory of the Soderini Garden: a piazza-garden that surrounds the ruin and hugs it like the houses demolished in the 1930s used to hug the lost Auditorium. An amenable, amicable, welcoming spot, *A Clean, Well-Lighted Place*, as in the title of a famous short story by Hemingway.

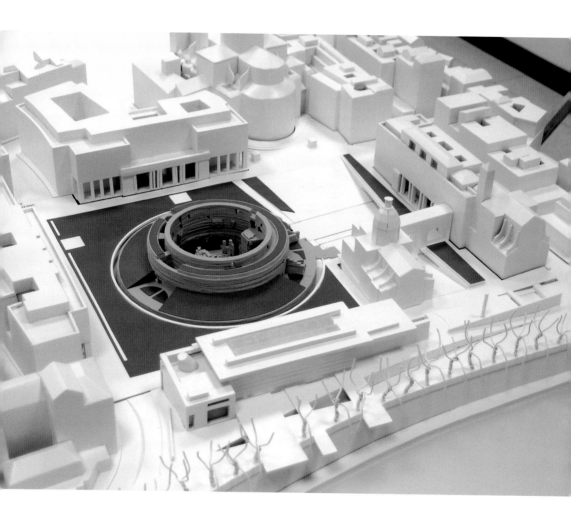

Previous pages: perspective view with the Church of San Rocco and the Church of San Carlo al Corso above, and the competition model. Below: competition perspective views.

Following pages: sections and interior plan of the Mausoleo di Augusto.

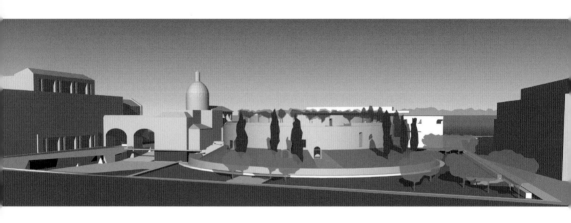

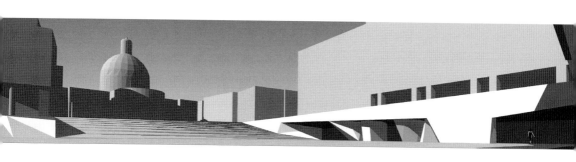

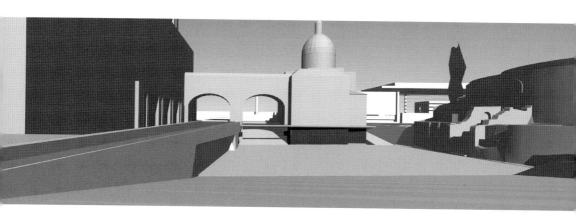

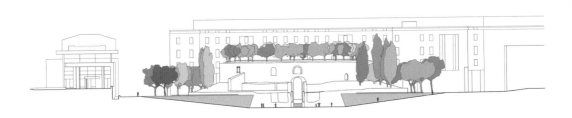

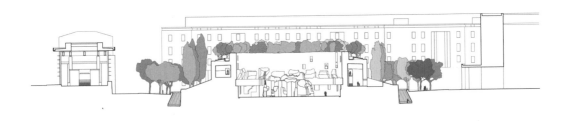

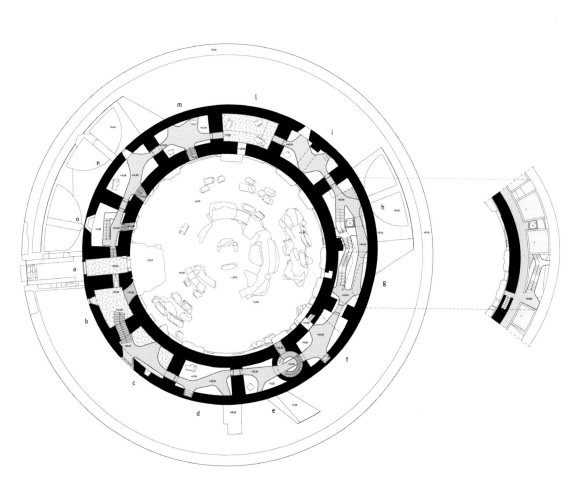

3

Bibliotheca Hertziana

Juan Navarro Baldeweg

In 1995, an invited competition was held for the re-modelling of the building containing the Bibliotheca Hertziana, a research institute on the history of Italian art associated with the Max-Planck Gesellschaft zur Förderung der Wissenschaften. The institute is located in an urban block extending from Piazza Trinità dei Monti and bordered by Via Sistina and Via Gregoriana. It comprises three building units: the sixteenth-century Palazzo Zuccari, Palazzo Nuovo (object of the redevelopment project), and the nineteenth-century Palazzo Stroganoff. The Palazzo Nuovo is the fruit of successive additions beginning in the latter half of the sixteenth century and continuing through the 1960s. It has transformed the once open garden of Palazzo Zuccari, accessed via the monumental Mascherone portal, into a closed volume that is out of tune with the historical fabric and completely lacking in adequate fire protection systems. The impossibility of storing newly acquired bibliographic materials in a facility that is not safe led the directors of the Max-Planck Society and the then director Cristoph Frommel to commission a new architectural project that would both resolve the safety code issues and provide greater long-term storage capacity. This effectively required the near complete demolition of Palazzo Nuovo.

The winning project took its cues from the history of the location, and shaped a contemporary fragment that recaptures the sense of space that used to characterize the site. The plans entail a system of jutting balconies around a glass prism that encircles the void of the former sixteenth-century garden. The new structure is a light machine lowered into the composition and exhibiting clear architectural independence. This formal design seeks to revitalize an array of different visual prospects, similar to those that once existed onto the garden both from Palazzo Zuccari and from the Mascherone portal, which is now rehabilitated as the new entrance to the library.

The balconies recede upwards in an allusion to the monumental system of exedra-like terraces, partially conserved beneath the library, of the Villa of Lucullus, which stood on the slopes of the Pincio from the first century b.C. to the first century a.C.

As it moved into the executive phase, the design contest transformed into a challenge for engineers to protect the site's archaeological heritage. This was accomplished by supporting the entire building on a pre-stressed slab supported in turn on two narrow piling walls under the current sidewalks of the sixteenth-century streets, leaving the entire area under the building free of foundations. This bridge system allows investigation of an unexplored part of Rome's archaeology while construction work is being carried out on top of the slab.

Left: view of Palazzo Zuccari on Via Gregoriana with the *mascherone*. Right: views of the model.
Pages 54-55: cross section, ground floor plan and model.
Pages 56-57: model highlighting the internal structure, sketch, and view of worksite.

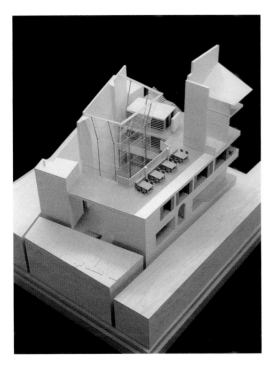
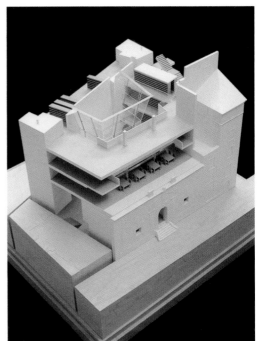
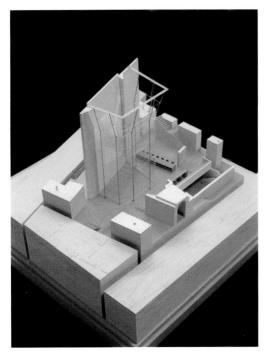
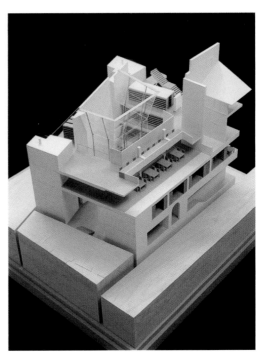

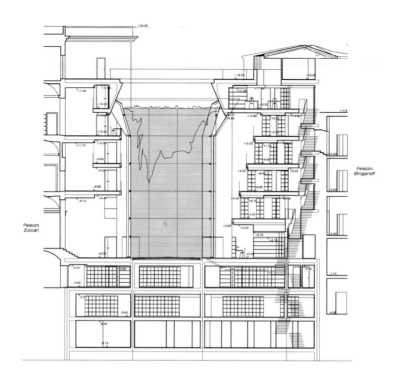

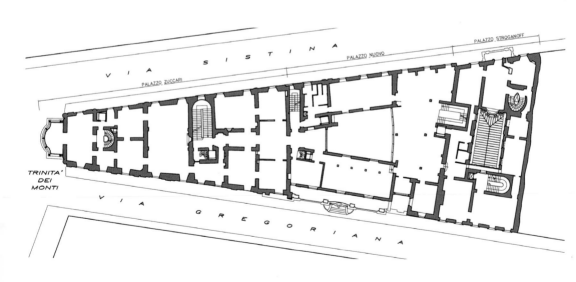

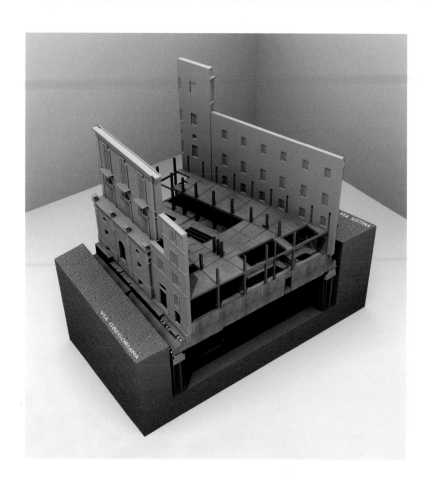

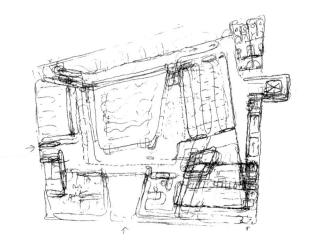

56

4

Museum Walkways
at the Mercati Traianei

Nemesi Studio

The project is part of the strategy of the City of Rome to transform the entire monumental complex of the markets into a permanent museum dedicated to the architecture of the Roman Imperial Age.

By opening itself to the city, the museum loses the closed dimension typical of classical architecture. The project consists in outfitting as museum spaces all the *tabernae* of the old market opening onto Via Biberatica, the urban axis of the new museum, and in installing a suspended pedestrian path over the ruins of Trajan's Forum, connecting Via dei Fori Imperiali to the Salita del Grillo.

Adopting the surface as an 'archetypical' element of the contemporary era, using the dynamism of signs and symbols, and presenting materials in their true identity, body is given to open objects, whose morphology cannot compete with but rather exalts the massive stereometric characteristics of the monument, in which the visual and material aspects prevail.

The bridge emerges from the deformation and bending of two surfaces in corten steel. It follows a trajectory over the Trajan Markets while engaged in a continuous process of transformation, and thus resolves the technical and structural problems as they arise. The walkway hangs light in the air, leaving the pattern of the ancient walls visible and readable and engaging the visitor in the archaeological landscape.

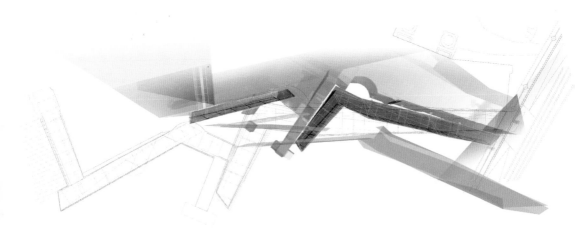

Previous pages: axonometry
and view of the walkways.
Bottom: views of the walkways.

5

Museum Space in the Campidoglio

Carlo Aymonino

In 1993, the commission considered the construction of a roof over the Giardino Romano based on the model of the old hall designed by Virgilio Vespignani in 1876 and demolished in 1902 during excavation work of the temple of Jupiter Capitolinus. The new hall was to contain the fronton and a reconstructed portion of the naos of the temple of Apollo Sosianus, and a newly revealed part of the wall of the temple of Jupiter Capitolinus that had been hidden behind walls erected in the early twentieth century.

The project at that time ideated a steel and glass structure, a hall appropriate for containing the recomposed pieces of the temple of Apollo Sosianus, which were approximately 17 metres high. The roof over the hall was composed of an open-weave steel trusswork that curved to form a self-supporting, dual module wall toward the Caffarelli garden. But the necessary archaeological investigations had not yet been carried out, and ten billion lire (approximately 6.5 million dollars in 1993) had been set aside for this task. Exploratory excavations were conducted from 1996 to 1999. The foundation wall was discovered and the upper Roman wall, already limiting the Caffarelli garden, was excavated.

Then the plan changed: no longer Apollo Sosianus but now Marcus Aurelius. Furthermore, the foundation walls of the temple of Jupiter Capitolinus were im-

pressive enough to merit exhibition. The arrival on the scene of the equestrian statue of Marcus Aurelius tilted things in favour of a spatial structure with strong visible polarity, as dictated by the imposing statue of the emperor (thus a geometric form was chosen that was closer to a circle than to a square or rectangle), and permitted a lower roof. The presence of the foundation wall, excavated on the front side down to its base (7 metres down), favoured a more complex spatial structure that exalted the vertical section and the site strata, a prerogative of the identity of the city of Rome.

Designs were finalized and the project was built in the years 1999 to 2005. The ellipse was chosen as the final form, not casually derived from the form of Piazza del Campidoglio. The edge of the ellipse is cut where it intersects the foundation wall of the temple of Jupiter Capitolinus, introducing a dynamic element into the space of the hall and drawing attention to the extraordinary archaeological relic of the Roman wall.

The space is made spectacular by the cavea and by an architectonic device of a lower ceiling over the tiers. The bearing structure is composed of steel pillars 70 centimetres in diameter. The protection against the elements is composed of triangular panels of structural glass. Technical systems are installed on the walls. The floor of the elliptical section is in Venetian cement and the stairs are in travertine stone.

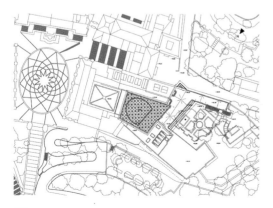

Left: plan with Piazza del Campidoglio on the left.
Right: roof of the Giardino Romano seen from neighbouring rooftops.
Pages 64-65: the interior with the equestrian statue of Marcus Aurelius.
Pages 66-67: sketches and view of interior space.

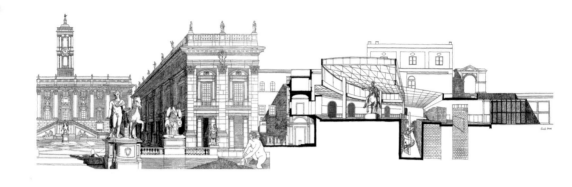

6

Reconstruction of the ex Serra Piacentini at the Palazzo delle Esposizioni

ABDR

The project ensures concrete feasibility to the glasshouse in terms of climate control, construction technology, operation and maintenance costs, and connections to the Palazzo delle Esposizioni (Palaexpo), in respect the architectural and monumental characteristics of the pre-existing building. The project will produce a quality structure in terms of materials, functional characteristics, and overall efficiency. The adopted architectural languages are based on overall simplification in order to minimize any direct conflict with the historical forms and languages of the Palazzo delle Esposizioni and eliminate any technological exhibitionism. At the same time, a work mimicking the architectural languages of the Palaexpo was rejected in the conviction that the nature of the new structure must be firmly anchored in current engineering, materials and construction culture.

Rather than exhibiting its own languages, the variant project seeks to maintain respect for the completeness of the volumes and the decorative divisions of the Palazzo delle Esposizioni by means of removal and minimalism. In short, today, an exaltation of Pio Piacentini's text can only be accomplished by abstaining from trying to create any new Piacentinian models. The glasshouse becomes an opportunity for reconnecting to Via Piacenza and an instrument for initiating a process of redevelopment and enhancement of a part of the city that has too long remained the 'backside' of the Palaexpo. This is a strategy, for that mat-

ter, that Piacentini himself favoured. He foresaw a dialogue between the glasshouse and the 'twinned' pavilions set up in the gardens of Via del Quirinale.

The organic quality of the interior has contributed to the achievement of these objectives. The inner volume is based on transparency and appropriate functional and technological choices. Externally, the succession of materials, moving from the masonry slab to the technical volumes faced in travertine stone, the glassed-in portion and the roof creates the effect of a progressive and measured dematerialization. The volume of the new glasshouse produces a delicate architectural and environmental equilibrium.

The volumetric simplicity and linearity of the project, together with the delicacy of the structure used to mount the glass panels, produce an effect of luminous inversion, symbolized in the contrasting appearances during the day and by night. The complete transparency achieved during the daytime by means of the large dimension glass panels and their system of stays offers completely new possibilities for those inside to observe the urban surroundings. At night, the dematerialized and luminescent prism of the glasshouse becomes a sort of 'urban lantern' that amplifies the expositional functions and communicative potentials of the Palaexpo, integrating them into the façade on Via Piacenza and thence into the nightlife along Via Nazionale, with the shops, theatres and other entertainment facilities.

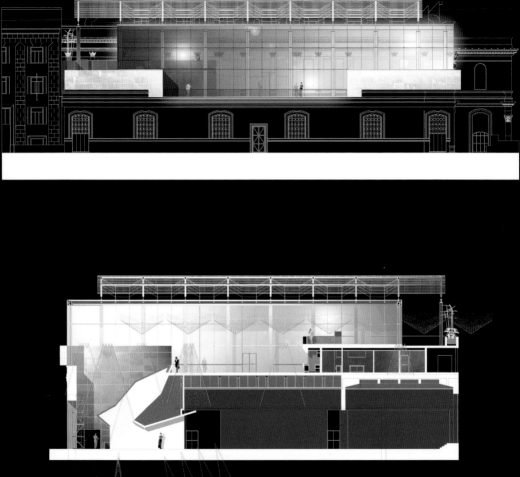

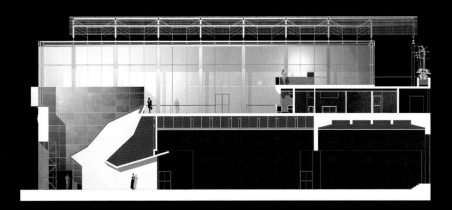

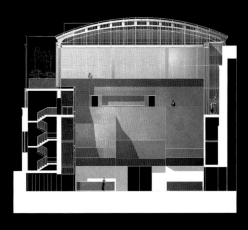

Pages 68-69: views of the
worksite and of the Serra
Piacentini from Via Piacenza.
Pages 70-71: elevation
and sections.
Below: first floor atrium.

The project forms part of a larger urban plan comprising the rest of the block and the surrounding blocks with the ambition of raising the area to a level in keeping with its central position in the city. This urban plan consists of moving an open market from the perimeter of an nineteenth century piazza into two former barracks, reactivating a theatre that had fallen into disuse, and generally restoring the area to its nineteenth century status. The site of the hotel was sold as an empty lot with a project ready for construction which had the twofold function of partially financing the rest of the urban scheme and secondly absorbing entirely the parking requirements of the area.

At first one reworked the basic design of a hotel over a car park into a project with more emphasis on the hotel and less on the carpark. As the site was cleared to start work on the foundations of this revised design, ancient Roman remains emerged over half the site. This brought the construction to an abrupt halt; archaeologists began excavations, and gave us the chance to propose a new design which obviated the need for so much underground parking. The urban landscape commission required us to turn the two completely different activities, namely a multi-storey car park and a hotel, into a unified block, entirely suspended from the ground, to allow access to the ruins on one half of the site and to the public areas of the hotel on the other half.

These public areas are generated by curved or folded planes that emerge from the level of the ruins; they house the conference hall, the saloon and the entrance lobby with access both directly from the street and through revolving doors of the main entrance on the south side. The curved plane is used again for the roofline under which the other principal public spaces are located: the restaurants, the bar and the fitness centre, all surrounded by generous terraces.

From the Esquilino hill, one of the highest in Rome, the views from the terraces command a panorama of the whole of the north, south and east of the city. The wooden decking of the terraces give a very strong sense of being on a moving ship. The courtyard is urbanistically important; it is substantially open on one side, to avoid the dark atmosphere of tall closed courtyards, and to connect the interior of the block with the public garden to the east and the theatre beyond.

Architecturally, the project has to do with the play of volumes originating in the 2 kilometers travertine wall of the station north of the building. This reference is reinforced by the use of a special plaster mix with a travertine color, which in time and with the help of the smog and the reddish rail dust will become part of the station complex.

The other strong exterior feature is the basalt base wedge on the north-east corner and the socle on the south-west, a material specified for all the pavements in this area. Here, the pavement is folded up to form the wedge; a device that masks the level differences on one elevation and forms a secondary entrance from the station on the other. The basalt socle, on the other corner, forms a base around what is effectively a massive bridge over the area of the ruins.

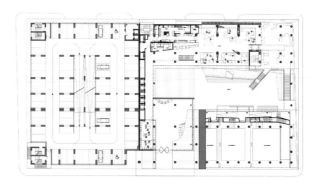

Pages 74-75: ground floor
plan and night-time view
of the atria.
Pages 76-77: the façade
on Via Giolitti.
These pages: external view
with the Stazione Termini
on the right, and external,
interior and detailed views.

8

Remodelling of the ex Ferdinando di Savoia Barracks

5+1AA

The building will house the new administrative offices of the Ministry of the Interior. The form of its worksite and excavation, its dimensions as a dinosaur of the Umberto I epoch and the public spaces embedded within it, brings out AMOR, the underground ghost town, mirror image of ROMA. The total white of the spaces represents a new world: sensual, floating and otherly, disorienting and surprising.

Given its strategic position, the barracks complex represents an urban connection node between the Termini Station and the Castro Pretorio, an area with important public functions (ministries, university, national library, etc.). The complex is part of the consolidated city adjacent to the Roman walls, characterized by a fabric comprising large monofunctional areas. Placed near the station but on the other side from the centre, it is marginal to the system of axes that connects the historical city to the station.

The complex is composed of ten buildings, five of which belong to the original barracks (1895) and the others built more recently (1960s-1990s). The main buildings (A, B, C) form a continuous and unitary C-shaped

unit enclosing the main courtyard. As often occurs in such buildings, architectural elements of great richness are intermixed with lower quality distributive solutions installed in later years.

The project objective was to emphasize the aspects of richness and monumentality by recovering and incorporating architectural elements associated with the access points, horizontal and vertical circulation, and the common spaces. The stair towers were redesigned to increase their monumental power: the straight and curving flights penetrate and cut through open spaces for the entire height of the building.

The project revolves around the functional needs. The recovery of the lower floors of the buildings, the demolition of surfeits, and the demolition and reconstruction of the roof with the addition of a fifth floor were all dictated by needs that are both quantitative (an increase in surface area to accommodate an increase in employees) and qualitative (space, natural and artificial lighting, differentiation between collective an individual work spaces, office hierarchy, circulation routes).

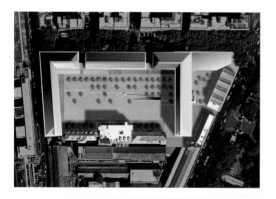

Left: roof plan. Right:
transparent rendering
of the distribution system.
Following pages: stairways.

9

Pontificia Università Lateranense
Extension of the Pio IX Library

King Roselli Architetti

Rector Monsignor Rino Fisichella made clear his intentions regarding the new library of the Pontificia Università Lateranense: make the consultation and reading space a pivotal point for the university. The university's collections number some 600,000 books, some dating back to the sixteenth century, mostly on philosophy, theology and canonical law. Many of the volumes are stored in recently renovated underground facilities; 25,000 old texts are kept in a protected environment. The library reading room was originally located on the first floor, which now houses the foyer of the Aula Magna (Great Hall) and the offices.

The new reading room and the books available for open consultation are now in a new building closer to the centre of the university and easily accessible from the main corridor on the first floor. Previously, there were a number of scattered reading rooms in different points of the university; they are now concentrated in a single volume, a six floor library tower containing 70,000 books and 750 publications.

The pivotal importance within the university of the library, archives and reading rooms is exemplified in the new building and in its location. The architectural volume of the library is discreetly aligned with the existing building and uses the same facing brick. But it vigorously affirms its modern identity: suspended volumes, contrast between light and shadow, clean cuts between voids and solid volumes. A stone loggia had to be demolished to make room for the new library. The university connects to the library via passageways that used to be windows to the outdoors, and the openings to the library tower are screened by means of glass partitions. A stairway made of basalt leads from the first floor of the university to the first level of the library. There, in the foyer, we find the computerized library catalogue, lockers, the reading room for professors, and the book distribution counter.

Three ramps with reading desks correspond to the six floors of the library tower. Each ramp connects two floors. The floor heights in the stacks are minimal in order to avoid high shelves, thus obviating the need for footstools or ladders to reach the books. Furthermore, the six levels are connected by means of a traditional stairway. The thinness of the floors, mimicking that of a bookshelf, transforms the tower itself into a huge bookcase.

The slope of the ramps connects the library tower to the irregular cuts in the façade, creating the reality (not just the effect) of a volume floating in light. During the day, the recessed design of the windows allows a mere glimpse of the faceted ceiling and the four support pillars. By night, the three main blocks float on blades of light. The ramps are not suspended in the void but defined by the vertical light that enters from the central skylight above and horizontally by the cuts in the two external façades. The landings on the ramps accommodate two reading desks, both made of solid mahogany. The ambient lighting fixtures are set into the desks. Lighting variations are very evident over the course of the day: the morning light enters directly through the façade windows and blends with the cooler, zenithal light descending from the overhead skylight. This overhead light warms towards midday and cools again into the afternoon. In the evening, it blends with the warm light of the sunset reflecting off the surrounding buildings. The layout of the ramps follows the dynamic shifts in lighting.

The project is also the structural response to a series of architectonic constraints imposed by the patient and brilliant engineer Andrea Imprenda: few pillars, minimum floor thicknesses, and foundations that leave the ruins of an underlying Roman villa virtually undisturbed.

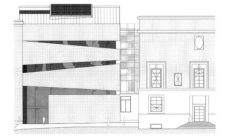

These pages: elevation and view of main façade. Pages 86-87: typical floor plan, cross section, view of library interior space. Pages 88-89: views of the library interior space from below and toward the floors with open shelving.

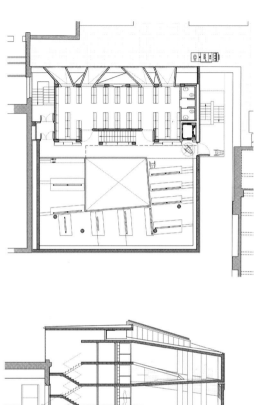

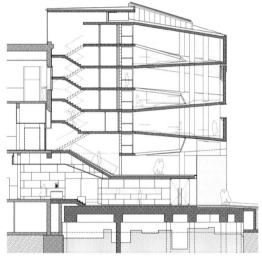

Rome Semicentre

10

MAXXI – Museo nazionale delle arti del XXI secolo

The Office of Zaha Hadid

The MAXXI addresses the question of its urban context by maintaining a connection to the former army barracks; it continues the low-level urban texture set against the higher level blocks on the surrounding sides of the site. The MAXXI is an 'urban graft,' a second skin to the site. At times, it affiliates with the ground to become new ground, yet it also ascends and coalesces to become mass where needed.

The building has an urban character: prefiguring upon a directional route connecting the river to via Guido Reni, the MAXXI encompasses both movement patterns extant and desired. This vector defines the primary entry route into the building. By intertwining the circulation with the urban context, the building shares a public dimension with the city, overlapping tendril like paths.

The move from object to field is critical, to understand the relationship architecture will sustain with the artworks it will house. The drifting emerges both as an architectural motif, and as a way to navigate through the museum. Paths lead away from the 'object' and its correlative sanctifying, towards fields of multiple associations. In configuring the possible identity of this newly established institution (housing both Art and Architecture), with its aspiration towards the polyvalent density of the twentyfirst century, conceptions of space and indeed temporality are reworked.

In architectural terms, this is executed by the figure of the 'wall.' Against the traditional coding of the 'wall' in the museum as the immutable vertical armature for the display of paintings, or delineating discrete spaces to construct 'order' and linear 'narrative,' we propose a critique of it through its emancipation. The 'wall' becomes the versatile engine for the staging of exhibition effects. In its various guises—solid wall, projection screen, canvas, window to the city—the exhibition wall is the primary space-making device. By running extensively across the site, the lines traverse inside and out. Urban space coincides with gallery space, exchanging pavilion and court in a continuous oscillation under the same operation. Walls emerge as incidents, becoming floors, or twisting to become ceiling, or are voided to become large windows.

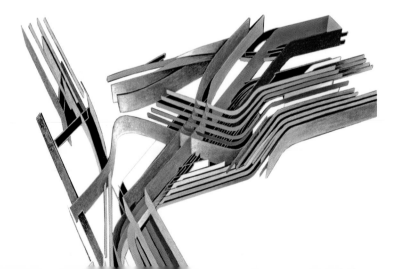

Previous pages: rendering
of volumes, and worksite
seen from above.
Right: interior view prior
to roof construction.
Following pages:
view of entrance and interior
view during roof construction.

The B1 Line, a branch of the currently existing Line B of the Rome underground railway system, will have four stations along its total length of approximately 4 kilometres.

Plans for the Gondar and Annibaliano stations have been modified with respect to those submitted to the design contest in order to improve their integration into the urban fabric by eliminating the aboveground volumes.

The Annibaliano station is laid out among the sinuous forms of an underground piazza. It is a broad space open to the sky that constitutes a new architectural pivot point, represents an urban redevelopment project, and provides a new hub for the city. A large open-air piazza is accessed via a gradual descent from the sidewalks of Corso Trieste that then provides access to the actual foyer of the station. This sublevel solution drastically reduces any volumetric clash with the adjacent mausoleum of Santa Costanza.

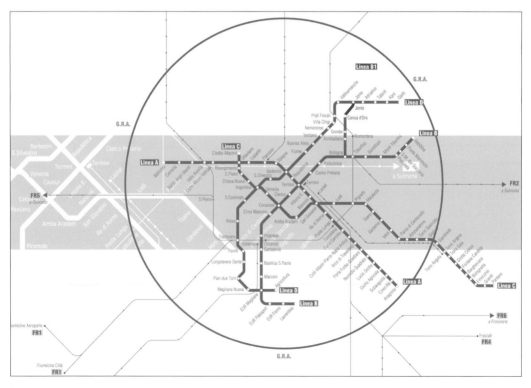

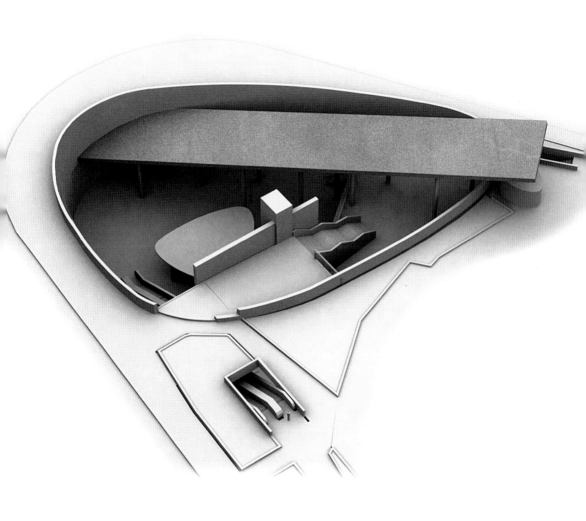

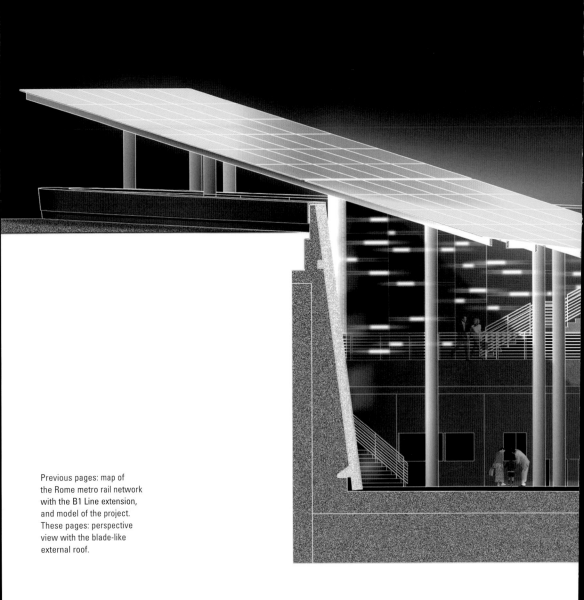

Previous pages: map of
the Rome metro rail network
with the B1 Line extension,
and model of the project.
These pages: perspective
view with the blade-like
external roof.

101

12

MACRO – Museo d'Arte Contemporanea

Odile Decq Benoît Cornette
Architectes Urbanistes

Because of the complexity of introducing a contemporary art gallery in an ancient mixed industrial building, the MACRO is an opportunity to transgress an univalent attitude of integration into a historical context. The new gallery makes the existing static condition of the site resonate with dynamism, movement and evidence.

In the gallery the section is shown through the translation from horizontal to vertical, from inside to outside, from the foyer to the roof-landscape-garden. The old and the new, the exhibition spaces and the other activities connected with it, are both articulated and distinct; in this system of transition the new contaminates all around, and every part becomes clear and attractive; the sequential discovery becomes event: to find the point of rupture, the transgression of the limits, and the quest for instability.

The MACRO is an experience of sensations, made of lines, surfaces, folds, and sections. The floor and the roof are engraved, fractured, open and animated by tectonic movements which give opposite directions for displacements and connect and articulate inside and outside spaces. On the two floor and roof surfaces, the structure of the existing building introduces grid and frame as places of stability. The open garden/terrace is perceived as a vertical axe of rotation from where the inside and outside, horizontal and vertical folds proceed.

The roof surface is a landscape, creating an outside/inside continuity. The roof is an abstract art garden: glacier, moor, aerial zoom view of Mars, graphic or geometric composition of light; it offers many textures under the feet of the visitors: rough, deep, smooth, soft, dense, bright, mat. The central volume of running water refreshes the air; over the centre of the foyer, it creates a sensation of freshness by evaporating during the heat days.

Pages 102-103: perspective
views of the conference
room and of the façade
on Via Reggio Emilia.
Previous pages: internal
view during construction.
These pages: perspective
views of roof, interior
and details.

13

New Rome Tiburtina
High Speed Station

ABDR

The winning project of the international design contest held by the Italian Rail Network for the New Tiburtina Station is the perfect opportunity to establish a new urban hub that connects, both spatially and physically, the Nomentano and Pietralata quarters, which had been isolated from one another by the rail lines. The new station, characterized by a bipolar design, establishes various interchange functions: road-rail, public-private, urban-extra urban. Additionally, it accommodates a complex system of administrative, commercial, hospitality and cultural functions as dictated by the Structure Plan, covering a total of 48,000 square metres.

The project is rooted in the local lines and axes and uses them to reconnect the new station to the physical reality of its two parent contexts. The pedestrian overpass over the railway bed makes it not only a bridge-station, but also a covered city boulevard providing not only intermodal exchange but also urban circulation and opportunities for socializing. The spatial concept is em-

bodied in a large container enveloping suspended volumes with an average dimension of 300 square metres that offer prestige functions such as a VIP lounge, an Internet office, private offices and restaurants. The characteristics of the volumes are coherent with the structural brief, which suggest a 'suspended' layout. This choice optimizes the structural spans of the upper floors, eliminating the critical conditions deriving from vibrations transmitted to the structure from the rail traffic and enhancing the interior bio-climatic conditions.

The urban system constituted by the ascending and descending piazzas ends towards the Nomentano with the vertical screen composed of the walls of the State Railway offices; at the centre of these offices, sloping at approximately 30 degrees, the bridge of the new railway station emerges into the urban space. On the Pietralata side, an urban foyer connects the urban function with the nascent administrative functions in this eastern sector of the city.

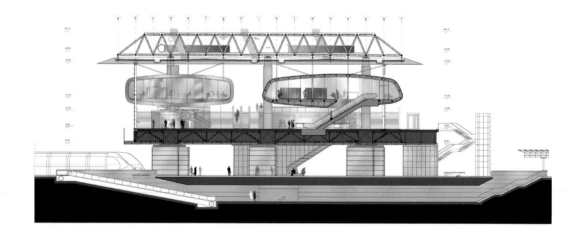

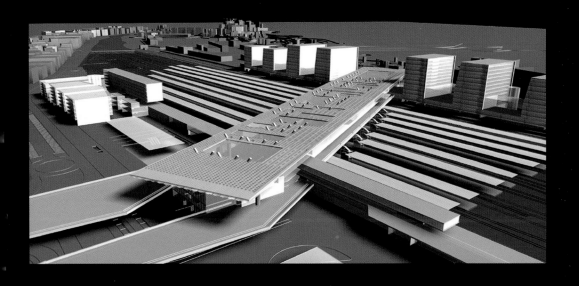

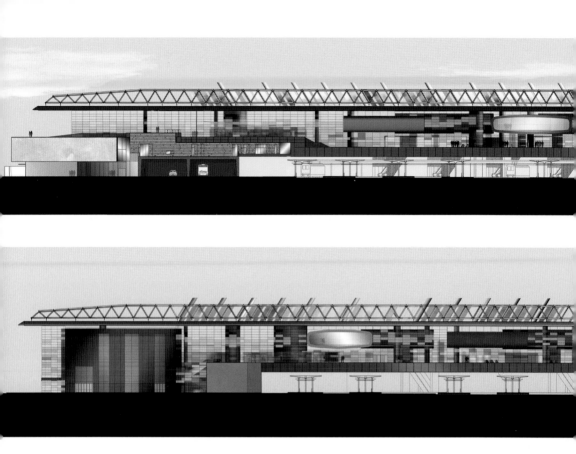

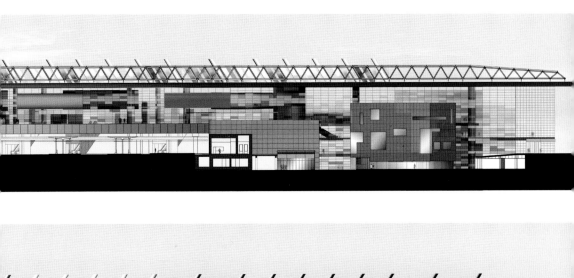

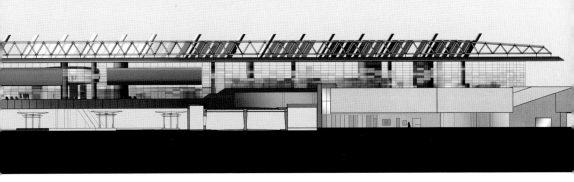

This project falls within the development of ATAC (Public Transport Municipal Authority) depots launched by the Municipality inside the city. The programme also envisaged the localization of offices, sales areas and dwellings.

The project consists in the urban restructuring of an area with a weak identity but with a high potentiality since it is placed on the 'edges' of the consolidated city.

In this framework, the project has a two-fold target: on the one hand, it aims at creating a new urban centrality, even if at the local level, on the other hand it aims at confirming the site identity as a place of transition, a privileged access to the consolidated city.

The project is structured on the design of a *porous* and *crossable* fabric able to identify a new complex and articulated urban area. The choice to design a fabric stemming from the directions and flows of the city results from the will and firm belief that the city must *not be built through objects but through systems*.

That is why the open spaces are never residual; the system of public areas and the one of built areas are integrated with the project; the *basement* becomes the bearing structure of paths and a path itself; as in the fabric of historic cities, the urban area becomes complex and rich, it spurs to run through it, to find it out; it finds in it the expression of collective values and the richness of individual paths.

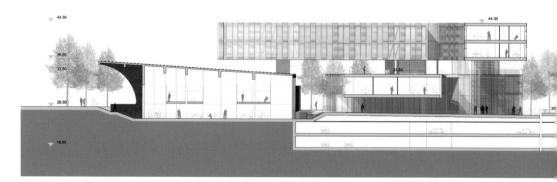

Previous pages: perspective
view from a high terrace
and section.
Above: overall perspective
view.

MACRO Future and Altra Economia at the Mattatoio

Luciano Cupelloni

The Mattatoio of Testaccio originally was a slaughterhouse, built in 1888–91, representing one of the large-scale public works in the reorganisation of primary urban services that took place soon after Rome became the new Italian capital. The slaughterhouse complex was closed in 1975.

In December 2000, the Ostiense Marconi Urban Project took form with the goal of establishing a 'City of the Arts.' The public initiative programme, guided by the City of Rome, included the participation of the University of Roma Tre, the Roman Museum of Contemporary Art (MACRO), the Roman Fine Arts Academy and the National Academy of Dance, Palaexpo with Zone Attive, the Testaccio Public School of Music, the Superintendencies and a host of cultural associations.

In parallel, the projects and initial temporary works of the MACRO Future and the workshops of the Fine Arts Academy were put into motion. As things stand today—the MACRO projects are completed, the Pelanda dei Suini project is underway, the spaces of Altra Economia (Alternative Economy) are nearing completion, and the work on the projects of Roma Tre and the two Academies will soon be initiated. It is estimated that the 'City of the Arts' will be a reality within five years and a campus dedicated to artistic pursuits will be fully functional within ten.

The MACRO has recovered buildings of industrial architecture, reinterpreting the characteristics of the old slaughterhouses and finding ways to establish transverse relations between them in the central rectangular space. Two of the four slaughterhouses will be renovated as exhibition spaces. Measuring some 1,000 square metres, each space has cast iron pillars, roof trusses and a network of iron ceiling beams. The museum functions are organised into two different spaces: there is a central area exhibiting the original characteristics of the Mattatoio, and two entirely new areas above the meat-handling rails.

The Alternative Economy spaces address the themes of economic innovation. Spaces dedicated to organic farming, fair trade, ethical financing, responsible tourism and open-source software, as well as the 'bio-bar' and the 'bio-restaurant' create a new environment in the architectural framework of the former livestock stalls. The Alternative Economy is the centrepiece of a socioeconomic model termed 'città solidale' (solidary city). It encompasses new practices in tune with current social demands and principles of sustainability, and is based on collective participation and responsibility, organized on a non-profit basis but functioning within the economic system.

Previous pages: vintage postcard and overall view of the slaughterhouse complex prior to redevelopment. This page: functional scheme and plan of the Alternative Economy (Altra Economia):

in grey Comune di Roma, in yellow Università Roma Tre, in brown Accademia di Belle Arti and Accademia Nazionale di Danza, in green Soprintendenza Beni Architettonici and Soprintendenza comunale, in blue Associazioni culturali

Below: plan with the Parco del Testaccio below and the Tiber above. Right: interior of one of the two MACRO Future pavilions. Following pages: the Alternative Economy pavilions.

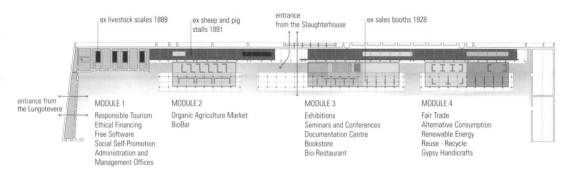

ex livestock scales 1889
ex sheep and pig stalls 1891
entrance from the Slaughterhouse
ex sales booths 1928

entrance from the Lungotevere

MODULE 1
Responsible Tourism
Ethical Financing
Free Software
Social Self-Promotion
Administration and
Management Offices

MODULE 2
Organic Agriculture Market
BioBar

MODULE 3
Exhibitions
Seminars and Conferences
Documentation Centre
Bookstore
Bio-Restaurant

MODULE 4
Fair Trade
Alternative Consumption
Renewable Energy
Reuse - Recycle
Gypsy Handicrafts

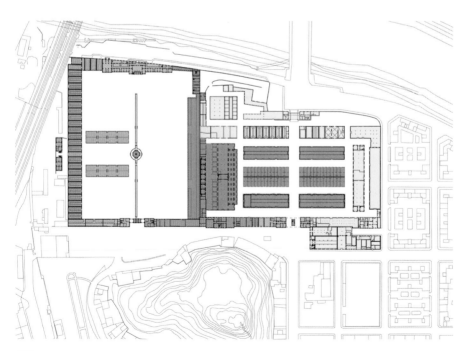

16

Headquarters of Italpromo & Libardi Associati

Labics

The project addresses the transformation of a school building to accommodate the new offices of Italpromo & Libardi Associati, an advertising and marketing agency. The project is located in the Ostiense quarter at the edge of the historical centre in one of the few industrial areas within the metropolitan territory. This industrial area is now undergoing its first significant urban, architectural and social transformation.

The project has two bases: the desire of the client to transform the interior space appropriately to meet the requirements of the new activities that will be taking place there, and the urban planning need to conserve the outer shell and outline of the building, which is now an integral part of the fabric of the district. This constraint became the node around which the characteristics of the project were developed. The building was transformed from within, literally gutted from the foundations to the roof. The liberated space was then gradually recomposed according to a new spatial organization and a new type of use.

The objective of the project is to bring innovation to office design after an investigation of the complex spatial, functional and social relations that establish themselves in a modern workplace.

Attention was dedicated particularly to the relationship between the group and the individual, between open space and individual spaces, and between production spaces and socialization spaces. In identifying the correct place for each activity, the entire building was broken down into three 'spatial systems' that divide it vertically: the void space of the public areas and circulation routes; the volumes of the meeting spaces and the individual work stations; and the neutrality of the open space.

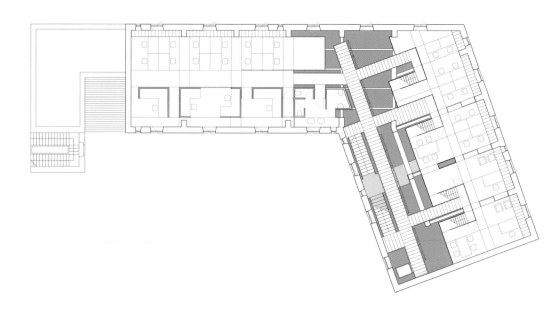

Previous pages: plan
and internal view.
These pages: the rooftop
volume with the gasometers
in the background, and interior
view.

17

Transformation of the Mercati Generali

OMA – Office for Metropolitan Architecture

The strategy for the redevelopment of the Mercati Generali proposes a balance of uses that closely resembles a method for the rehabilitation and reprogramming of disused structures. Whereas historically public space flourished around squares and streets linked to religious or civic buildings or landmarks, today's cities rely increasingly on the private sector to propagate the city pulse, especially through retail and leisure.

The present convergence of urbanity and commercial mega-structures questions the status of public space today. Where the later outgrows its envelope and overflows into the city as an independent instrument of urbanity, cities instigate regeneration resorting to commercial strategies. The redevelopment of the Mercati Generali offers the opportunity to define a balance between the two. The Mercati Generali site on the via Ostiense is a peculiar location in the fringe of the familiar Rome, only a few blocks from the ancient city walls. This central, yet edge location, offers a proximity that eases building inside Rome, with the apparent luster of being outside the Rome. The strategic location, historical importance, urban presence and shear scale of the Mercati Generali should be exploited to spearhead the redevelopment of the complete neighborhood.

Working with a historical site, almost a given in Rome, implies abiding to strict rules of intervention that are heavily prescriptive and severely limit the implantation of the new. In the case of the Mercati Generali the task becomes more so challenging given its relative youth (by Roman standards). Built from the early to mid 1900's, and its current state of 'limited' decay yet with 'substantial' historical documentation poses the challenge of practicing an industrial archaeology of great meticulousness offering minimal leeway.

Left: aerial view of the Mercati
Generali along Via Ostiense
with the Stazione Ostiense
at the upper right.
Right: model of the project.
Following pages: views
of the model and longitudinal
section.

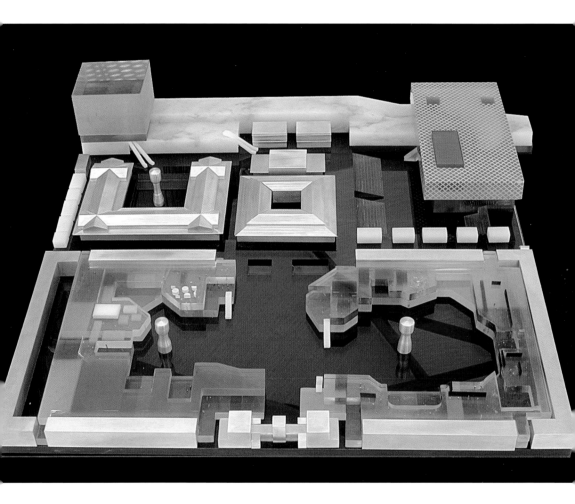

Rectorate, Faculty and Department of Law – Università Roma Tre

Giuseppe Pasquali, Alfredo Passeri

From 1909 to the 1980s, the area was occupied by a glassworks plant. It lies along Via Ostiense, opposite Schuster Park, next to the Basilica of San Paolo fuori le mura. The new building, accommodating the new Rector's office and the School of Law, is part of an urban programme for the renewal of a section of city that has witnessed important episodes in its pluri-millenary history: the necropolis around the Basilica of San Paolo, the Basilica itself, the pyramid of Caius Cestius, Porta San Paolo, the Testaccio neighbourhood (built in 1907–30), the post office designed by Adalberto Libera and Mario De Renzi in 1933–35, and the Garbatella district which was built in the 1920s.

The university complex stands on an area of some 19,000 square metres and is composed of two L-shaped buildings off which branch the lower units of the classrooms and common areas. The overall aboveground volume is 48,580 cubic metres, corresponding to a surface area of 14,520 square metres. Five thousand students attend the facility.

The L-shaped units accommodate the studies and offices of the Rector, the Faculty and the Department of Law, connected by a network of walkways located inside a full-height gallery that acts as an interrelational space.

The geometric network is composed of a square grid measuring 7.20 metres on a side.

There are nine classrooms, all on the ground floor: two seat four hundred and fifty students, six seat two hundred and forty, and the last one seats one hundred. The Great Hall contains two hundred and sixty seats.

From the Art Nouveau building on Via Ostiense, where the Rector's offices were located until the new project was completed, one gains access to an internal piazza (at an elevation of + 2 metres) outlined on two sides by a sequence of two-story-high pilotis and to the right by the cylindrical volume of the Great Hall. Here begins the large full-height gallery that leads to all the ground floor classrooms and contains the student study areas on the intermediate level. The gallery contains the elevated walkways that connect the departmental offices.

The external walls are made of few materials: bare brick, anodized aluminium door and window frames, zinc and titanium alloy panels for the cylindrical volume of the Great Hall, cement for the partition walls that outline the piloti level. The top of the building is a metal gridwork in galvanized sheet metal that conceals the machinery of the technical plants.

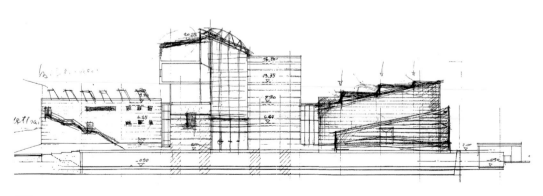

Below: sketches of the volumes
and of the gallery, and general
view from the railway lines.
Pages 134-135: the gallery
and Great Hall seen from
the entrance.

Pages 136-137: the gallery
and the Rectorate block.

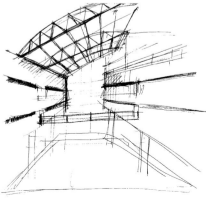

A completely virtual point in the area, site of a cross surrounded by greenery, where all the perspective lines generated by the volumes converge, the Church of the Santo Volto di Gesù is broken in two by a strong spatial and morphological mark represented by an open-air route, the 'luminous path' that leads towards the vanishing point of the cross, well beyond the building.

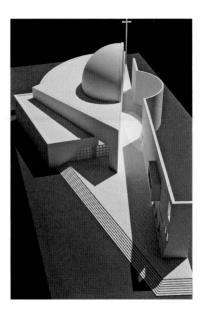

What are the origins of the architectural plan? It was necessary to exalt the potentials of the corner of Via della Magliana and its cross street, between the façade with the small buildings and the façade on the grand tree-lined avenue contiguous with the Tiber oxbow. The space by the created maximum divergence of the perspective lines is actually the church forecourt opening towards the road intersection. The forecourt is a V-shape simulating arms reaching out towards the city and suggesting an idea of the city as a *communitas* that penetrates into the sacred space. It is an urban void carved out of the solid mass of the built environment, a piazza uniting city and church.

The interior-exterior compositional epicentre comprises a virtual sphere that may be interpreted in plan as the sum of the external apse and the semi-circular internal podium. By a process of removal, the semi-cupola that would have covered the external space is gone; only one half remains indicating the hall where the sacred functions are performed, separated from the external apse by a large transparent diaphragm.

In the nave, the flat roof over the congregation hall is sliced by the vertical surge of the semicupola rising above the presbytery to the caesura with the large circular window to the rear. The semicupola is supported by a circular steel structure fixed to the straight wall of the nave that has a diameter of approximately 20 metres around an eccentric pivot. The volume of the place of worship has a monolithic appearance emphasized by the use of a single material, Roman travertine stone.

The vivacity of the layout, arranged around the atrium-piazza of the rooms, is mirrored in the volumes by the juxtaposition of intense and contrasting colours that exalt its organicity. The pathway of the gallery—linear diaphragm and vertical circulation space that connects the rooms, the auditorium, the parochial offices and the guest quarters—culminates at the space dedicated to the bells, which overlook the forecourt.

Previous pages: model
and external view
from Via della Magliana.
These pages: interior views.

20

Storehouse-Laboratory at Villa dei Quintili

n! studio

The building is in the Villa dei Quintili archaeological site, between Via Appia Antica and Via Appia Nuova. The site is currently an archaeological park open to the public.

The client's intention was to create a facility to be used for the collection, cleaning and restoration of archaeological relics unearthed in the digs.

The fundamental theme addressed by the project was the relationship between the site's historical context and the landscape. The nearby Roman cistern, the surrounding local vegetation, the visual impact of the building on the various skylines in which it participates, and even the ground on which it stands all contributed to determining the choice of materials. Two materials were used: glass and corten steel. The glass panels, installed without the use of a frame, create a front façade that either reflects the surrounding landscape or appears completely transparent depending on the lighting conditions. The corten steel covering the rest of the building will tend to blend in with its surroundings as it gradually forms its rusty patina.

The two long sides of the building present different architectural solutions. The more open side evokes the idea of the stacked crates of archaeological materials inside the building. The back side, which is necessarily more closed, is fragmented into many parallel lines by U-section profiles, relieving the generally long and low structure, similar to the nearby Roman cistern, of its sense of density.

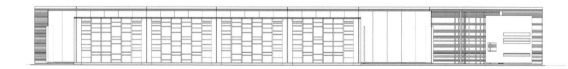

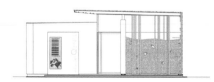

Previous pages: elevations
and view of rear façade.
These pages: site plan
and views of the entrance
side looking onto excavations.

21

Centro Congressi Italia at EUR   Massimiliano Fuksas

The building is a large longitudinally oriented translucent container standing 30 metres tall. There are open piazzas on either side giving onto the surrounding city. The former is engaged in a constant and direct dialogue with the neighbourhood and provides circulation pathways between Viale Europa and Viale Shakespeare; the latter, a space with moveable structures that allow it to be modified, receives and channels convention participants to the various halls of the Centre. Simple and perpendicular lines pay homage to the rationalist architecture of the 1930s that characterizes the physiognomy of the EUR and Adalberto Libera's Convention Centre.

'The idea came to me at a very particular moment. I was at the seaside and some clouds were moving by, blown along by a very fast wind. As I watched the clouds, one of my old dreams resurfaced: to create a building that was not crystallized into any form.'

Inside the Convention Centre, a steel and Teflon cloud measuring 3,500 square metres is suspended above a surface area of 10,000 square metres that accommodates an 1,800-person auditorium and an array of meeting rooms. The polyfunctional space of the Centre comprises a total of 15,000 square metres and has three halls and large spaces for foyers, cafés and restaurants. The cloud, supported by a dense network of steel ribs and suspended between the floor and the ceiling of the large illuminated hall, gives the building a vibrational appearance when viewed from afar, offering views that are always different and changing.

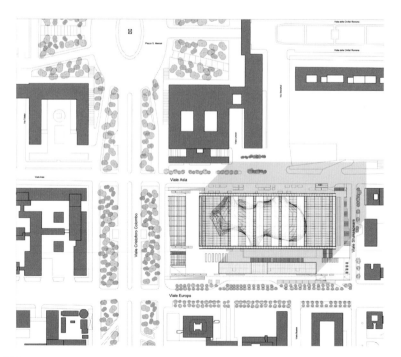

Left: plan. Right: interior view.
Pages 148-149, view from
Viale Cristoforo Colombo.
Pages 150-151, elevation,
sections and studies
of the cloud containing
the Auditorium.

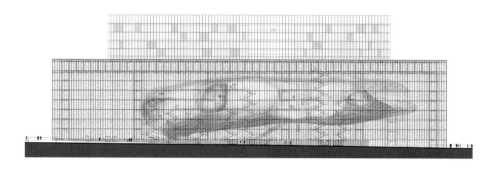

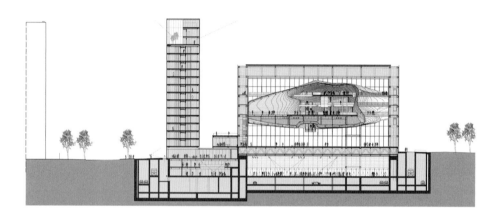

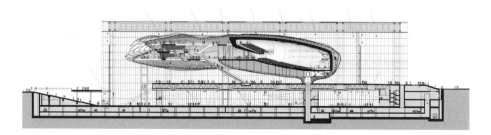

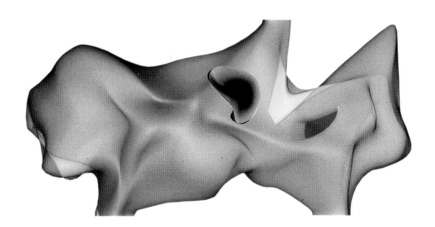

Rome Outskirts

22

Church of Santa Maria della Presentazione

Nemesi Studio

The project is part of the '50 churches for Rome 2000' programme undertaken by the Vicariate of Rome for the Jubilee; it consists in the creation of religious, cultural and sports facilities within the Quartaccio district, a 'marginal' portion of the metropolitan fabric on the northern outskirts. In contrast to 'true' parochial centres, which constitute the heart of the Jubilee programme, Santa Maria della Presentazione offers mixed functions, including facilities for liturgical functions (a ferial chapel, classrooms for catechism, parsonage) and facilities for cultural and sports activities (theatre works, public assemblies and, in exceptional cases, religious functions).

The project interprets the functional programme in a symbolic key and draws its power from the contrast between two architectonic organisms. The civic part is a 'presence'—a compact, abstract and introverted volume—that appears as an 'emergent' object belonging

to the surrounding landscape. The sacred part, vice versa, is configured as an 'absence,' the void constituted by the flat roof, the regular grid of pillars and the transparent plane that constitutes its shell. Together, these elements create an environment where the volumes dedicated to the single functions share in a dynamic interrelationship. This space, in its dual valence of interior and exterior, of fluid density, imploded but open to the landscape, finds its symbolic value in being 'matter' capable of bringing its loci into relation with one another and with their built and landscape context.

As a connecting element between the city and the open spaces typical of the Roman countryside, the project is set at an average elevation of 5 metres below road level, thus giving physical body to the condition of being marginal. At the lowest level there is a piazza, which acts as the functional fulcrum for the complex, a place for access and distribution of circulation flows.

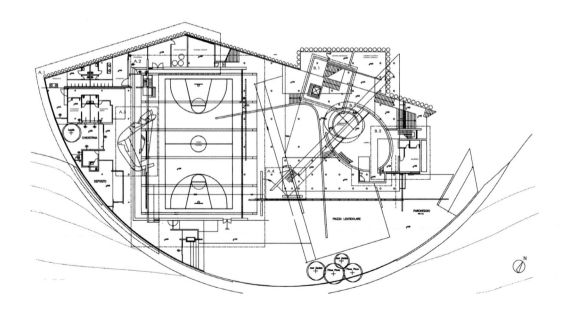

Previous pages: ground floor
plan and view of the entrance
space.
Below: the entrance side
and the rear side.
Following pages: details.

The Bufalotta urban plan lays out a new urban development along the Grande Raccordo Anulare (GRA) between the neighbourhoods of Val Melaina and Fidene-Castel Giubileo. The new section of city uses the landscape as the element to create relations among the parts, with a high percentage of public green land (approximately half of the 332 hectares of the plan). The central axis is a boulevard that winds its way east-west, intersected by secondary streets shaped like an eight. The intersections form nuclei with different uses. There are piazzas and widenings of the road that accommodate public facilities: theatres, hotels, a church and a healthcare centre. The service sector buildings on the main avenues and their residential counterparts reach a height of seven stories in certain nodal points, but for the most part are low density. The plan proposes elements of continuity that connect the built area with the surrounding territory, respecting the pre-existing elements and stitching them back together with the fragments of the surrounding outskirts, which are thus recontextualized in a new geography. The urban project locates the individual buildings in a shared horizon that is sufficiently flexible to accept future modifications, now providing norms for the outline of the plan and its density and controlling certain nodal points. The plan involves a new exit from the GRA at Via Settebagni and the extension of the road coplanar to the GRA that currently starts at the junction with the A1 Autostrada (Milano-Napoli) and will connect to Via delle Vigne Nuove. At the intersection of these two roads we find the Porta di Roma shopping centre, pivot point of the plan and a landmark for the neighbourhood. Studio Valle Architetti Associati has designed the entire centre, collaborated with the project manager (Ufficio Tecnico Imprese Lamaro) in developing the executive plan, and is in charge of artistic direction and image control. The parking facilities, concentrated on two levels for a total of 230,000 square metres, provide access to two levels of shopping arcades, a cinema multiplex, a tower with hotel, the IKEA and Leroy Merlin stores, and three pedestrian piazzas. Unlike many shopping centres that have external parking lots surrounding an isolated island of buildings, here all functions are concentrated in a single structure surrounded by perimeter roads. The structure is made of prefabricated cement elements and based on an 8 metre x 8 metre grid deriving from the spacing of the automobile lanes. The shopping arcades, with a usable area of some 150,000 square metres, form a multilevel city with its own internal public life. The roof is marked by skylights and natural light also illuminates the parking facilities by means of light wells. The skylights and the tower marking the entrance make the complex a landmark visible from afar. After arriving by car and entering the parking slab, one gains access to the shopping areas via the vertical circulation facilities in the vertical wells. The internal arcades then give access to the pedestrian piazzas and then to the various buildings in the centre, such as IKEA and Leroy Merlin. The building is not perceived as an architectural object, but as artificial orography.

Left: site plan.
Right: aerial view.
Pages 162-163: the IKEA buildings and the UGC multiplex.
Pages 164-165: exit from underground parking into the shopping centre.

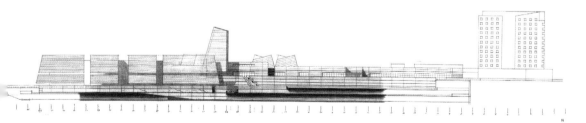

The mindset that would see the school as a castle of learning, separated and protected from the clamour of the outside world must be replaced by a vision of the school as a node in a network of educational, institutional and other functions that in all cases are public and within the purview of the local community. The relationship between the school and the surrounding environment flows in both directions, and the enrichment from the school amplifies the functions of the outer world, thus reflecting the encounter and integration of different habits and perspectives. The educational complex in Casal Monastero implements such a vision, employing architectural, environmental and urban planning devices that ensure its integration into the territory and respect for the activities in the community, flexibility in assignment and use of spaces, and a balance between public and private realms.

A representation of the complex of daily educational activities in the various areas highlights various situa-

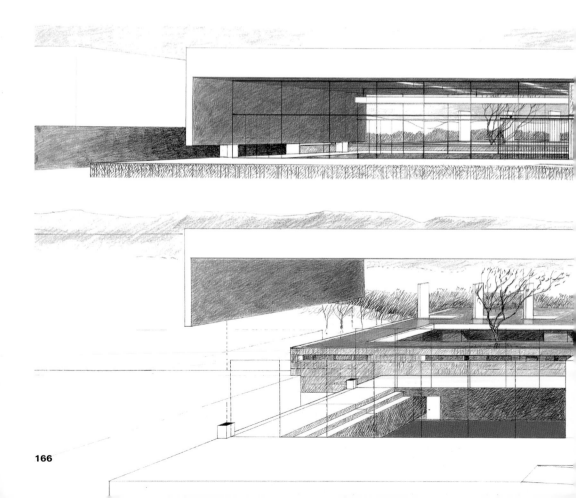

tions: the classroom, where collective activities are organized for small or large groups; the courtyard, where students and teachers can meet or seek a place for retreat or reflection; the special rooms for targeted supplementary education, projecting activities outside of the classroom where sports and encounters with the public take place; the circulation routes, panoramic points and meeting areas that exalt the transparency of the adopted pedagogic model. The scholastic complex manifests the dual purpose of the programme via two distinct volumes: a building providing services to the neighbouring community and a building for educational purposes. The former is characterized by high visibility, the latter by introspection and concentration. The form of the organism makes reference to abstract concepts: large hollowed stone blocks (basement) supporting slabs that determine a variety of spaces: the roof, the enclosure, the precinct, and the underground path.

Previous pages: perspective
views of the project.
Below: model, plan,
and interior perspective view.

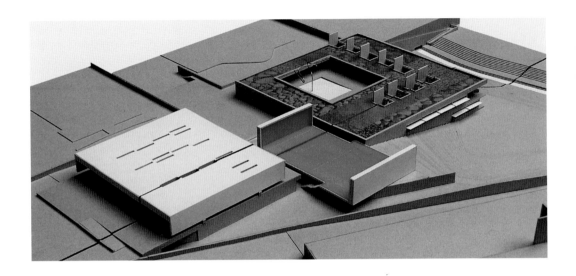

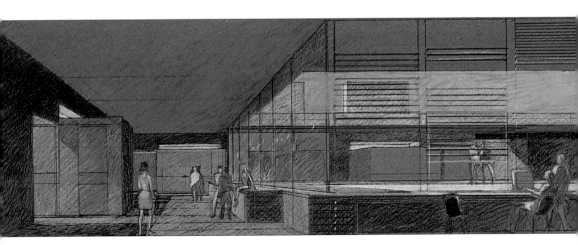

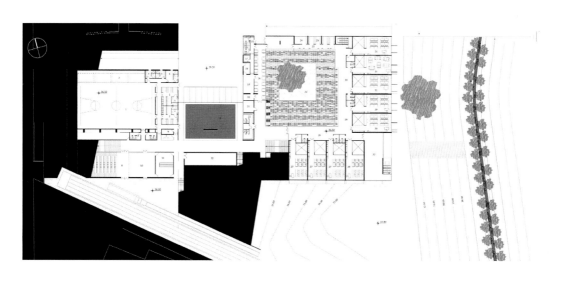

169

Church of Santa Maria Josefa

Garofalo Miura

The church stands on a square plot of land measuring eighty metres on a side between an area of illegally built structures and a low-income, subsidized housing development, at km 16 of Via Prenestina. The parochial centre is contained in an L-shaped building whose short side contains a two-hundred seat auditorium. The nave faces the neighbourhood and is surrounded on two sides by a large forecourt containing the bell tower, which emerges as an extension of the church façade.

The façade is characterized by a screen of white cement panels that filter the afternoon sun and allow it to penetrate into the depths of the church all the way to the presbytery. Taking advantage of the uneven terrain, the interior extends beyond the presbytery into a chapel on the lower floor, connected by stairs and ramps that 'detach' the plane of the church level from the ground and from its shell.

The square nave, austere in its forms and proportions, has a green marble floor and is panelled in cherry. The back wall of the presbytery marks out the succession of choir, tabernacle, altar and the area of the presbytery reserved for the celebrant in a broken progression.

The parochial centre itself is housed in the red building behind the church and contains the offices, apartments, rooms and the auditorium, which is partially discontinuous with respect to the building. The design of the exterior accentuates the introverted and monolithic character of the building, which seeks monumentality through a minimal articulation of the volumes and surfaces and by scaling up the elements that are normally built on the human scale.

Below: ground floor plan.
Right: external view.
Following pages: exterior
details and interior view
of the church from the altar.

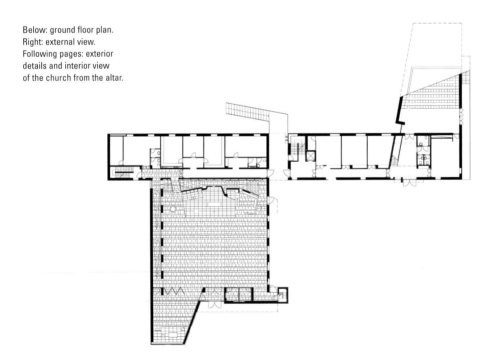

26

Tor Vergata University Laboratories

IaN+

The building is part of a scattered system of rural buildings converted to laboratories and departmental offices within the hydrobiology station of the University of Rome at Tor Vergata. The architecture engages in a process of interchange with the surrounding context. It is a simple element, a parallelepiped, which is subjected to the potential effects of deformation. The three-story building has a compact floorplan. The first two floors house the laboratories while the third contains a large meeting room that overhangs the access court.

The building merges the void of the vertical circulation system, the void created by the reversal of the roof slope and the solid comprising the laboratory spaces. The rough external surfaces are finished in a coarse grained stucco with colours that seek to mimic the rural buildings in the immediate vicinity.

Above and right: external views of entrance side. Following pages: elevation, section and view of rear side.

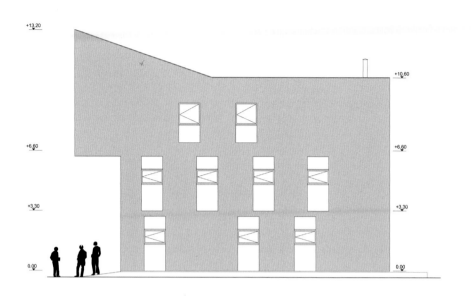

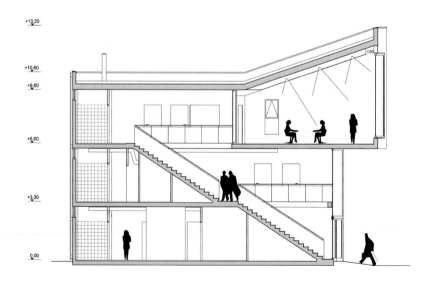

27

Church of Santa Margherita Maria Alacoque

Italo Rota & Associati

The church in Tor Vergata dedicated to Santa Maria Alaloque tells a tale woven of the nature of a religious space (whose highest meaning is in the ascension of the Madonna) and the coarse humanity of the landscape of the Roman countryside dotted with illegal buildings, pastureland and a mixture of vegetable patches. Like an ark that comes to rest on the earth, it does not modify it: it settles in and forms its own setting. It does not change the rules of the territory, but accommodates itself among them, respecting the pre-existing elements.

This is also the landscape where Pope John Paul II organized a large gathering and met with young Catholics for the Jubilee of 2000. The church, desired by the Curia in remembrance of that day, stands where the ceremony was held and recovers its ecumenical spirit. Its architecture re-evokes the spatial symbology of old churches, re-establishing the rule of their proportions. A central volume with a large nave reminiscent of rustic farm buildings rises skywards to signify the connection with the uppermost. An ark that connects the two banks of the strait that separates heaven and earth and contains the icons. A house of the Virgin that keeps the sacred bleeding heart.

Two levels, one earthly, the other heavenly, find elements of dialogue in a number of icons. The 'human' and earthly part is rooted in geometry, dug into the earth, where it uncovers an archaeological mosaic floor. Above, the veil of the Madonna, of the Virgin, forms a heavenly vault that embraces the church of the faithful.

Four transparent columns full of light rise from the floor and structurally connect the large window that brings in light from above, light filtering through golden film like a Byzantine heaven.

The volume of the church is flanked by a bell tower that contains the garden of the Virgin, the grotto, and a garden filled with flowers. This element is also dug into the earth in order to project the garden upward, where the grotto receives the Virgin Mother and gives a view of the heavens through the metal roof.

Left: view of entrance side.
Right: elevations and sections.
Following pages: view of the rear side.

SEZIONE L-L

SEZIONE M-M

SEZIONE D-D

SEZIONE F-F

SEZIONE A-A

SEZIONE B-B

28

School in Romanina

Located in a new area in a suburb, the complex consists of a combination of a 10-class primary school and a 6-class school preparing for secondary education. The teaching sections of both schools can be made separate and have separate entrances with play areas below the level of the surrounding land. The schools are grouped along a central axis—shifted one storey with respect to each other—on which the communal dining area and the communal open auditorium-like space are located.

The building comprises repeated basic units, blocks which can house four classrooms but have a flexible layout. Like traditional Roman houses these basic units are grouped around a patio. The building can be extended with more basic units.

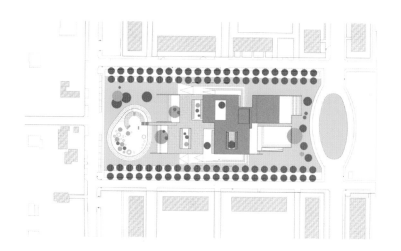

Previous pages: site plan
and perspective view
of the internal courtyard.
Above: perspective view
of the multifunctional space.
Right: longitudinal section.

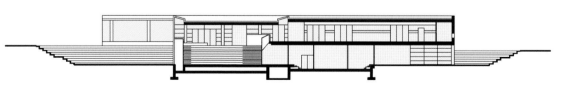

29

Defence Administrative Centre in Cecchignola

Marco Petreschi

The project is based on the decision of the central administration of the Italian Defence Ministry to rework a project for a new administrative centre initially developed by its own technical department. It was the Ministry's conviction that the project needed to be optimized in terms of environmental impact, in spite of the notable dimensions of the building, which would stand on the highest position of an area opening onto the Roman countryside. The building occupies a site facing a large residual area of the Cecchignola military base, well visible from the Grande Raccordo Anulare (GRA).

With respect to the forerunner project, the architectural elements of the elevations were reduced in order to emphasize a more compact and homogeneous morphology and image, opting for a continuous outer wall of brick. The impact of the building's emergence from the ground was attenuated by landscaping the external area. The brick outer walls are thus conceived as a succession of solid and void spaces giving continuity and rhythm to the overall project, thus making the massive wall appear to be a fragment of a Roman aqueduct, an artifact that is typical of the surrounding landscape. The openings are created by means of a few dimensional cuts. Given the notable dimensions of the complex, it was decided to accentuate the architecture of the central unit with a main entrance from the square on Viale dell'Esercito. Here a concave and perforated screen-wall in brick and travertine stone interrupts the serial modularity of the lateral façades. A convex element is juxtaposed with this screen that supports a canopy over a temporary parking area. On the inside, behind the screen, the open reception is a triple-height volume. A glass wall of giant proportions between the external wall and the atrium lets in light filtering through the holes in the screen-wall.

The project called for artificial hills (which were omitted from the final project) along the automobile routes and the base of the building, creating an undulating terrain like a theatre backdrop. This would have achieved an apparent reduction in the dimensions of the building and its footprint. Grass covered hillocks with a few copses of trees surrounded by shrubbery would have screened the service entrances to the climate control plant, the kitchens or other zones easily seen from the surrounding ground level.

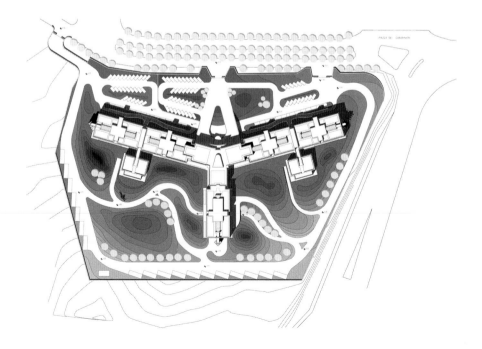

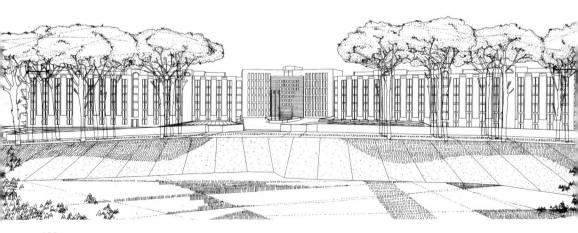

Previous pages: site plan
and view of the entrance
atrium.
Left: general and perspective
view of the entrance side.
Above: view of the rear side
facing the Grande Raccordo
Anulare.

The church as the 'house of the celebrant community' is composed of two parts that must have a clear relationship and immediate interpretation: the nave as the place for the congregation and the presbytery as the place where the rite is celebrated. An open relationship must be established between these two, not a separation between two different realms, but a close tie in which the one has no sense without the other.

For this reason, the presbytery opens to the nave and becomes an inseparable part, a space enclosed on three sides and open on the fourth, within which the liturgy is enacted. It is the space for the altar, the ambo, the seat of the officiating priest. It is the central area around which gravitates the entire surrounding space. This space is at the base of a tower. The walls of the presbytery rise beyond the roof of the room for the assembly of the faithful and receive light through a large skylight above.

The second element, the nave where the congregation assembles, is circumscribed by a nearly square fence that also encloses the presbytery tower. The faithful gather inside the enclosure, accessed via a large door along the central axis of the presbytery and by two side doors (as well as a secondary passage to the sacristy), and all activities of the liturgical function are distributed therein. The baptismal fount is on one side of the presbytery, the tabernacle for the Eucharist is on the other. Immediately next to the tabernacle stands the ferial chapel, which may also be used as a place for prayers. Visible from the congregation hall, the tabernacle sits between the ferial chapel and the presbytery so that it is easily accessible from either altar. The square enclosure that delimits the place of worship is illuminated from above and equally visible as the presbytery that it encircles and protects, as it protects the gathered faithful oriented towards it.

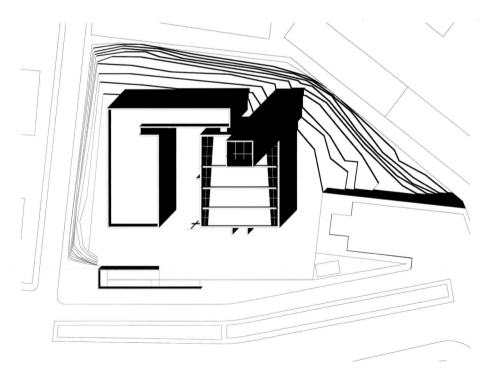

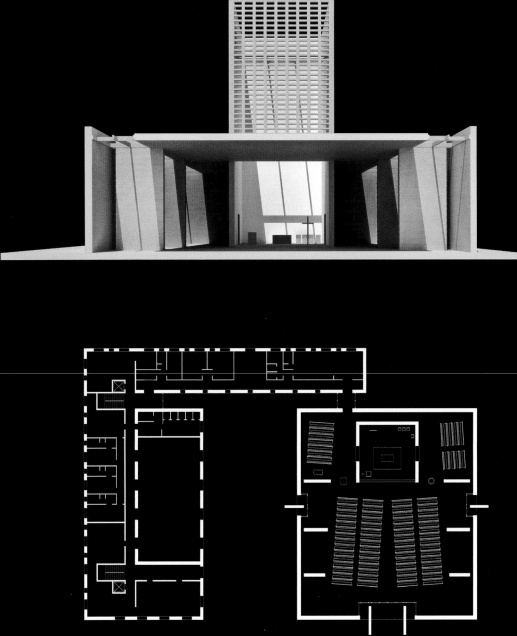

Previous pages: site plan, section and ground floor plan. This page: elevations and sections. Right: perspective view toward the altar.

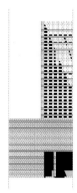
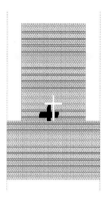

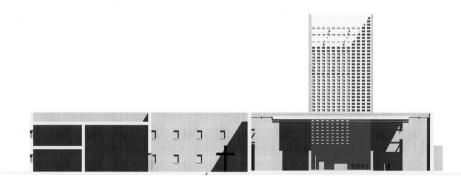

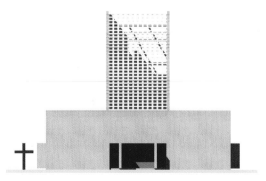
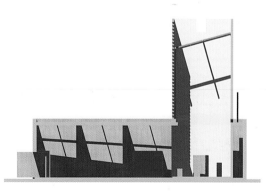

The site is located in the Infernetto quarter, a peripheral low-density residential expansion zone along Via Cristoforo Colombo between the Grande Raccordo Anulare (GRA) and the coastal town of Castel Fusano. The urban plan calls for full saturation along the main axis of Via Wolf Ferrari, shaded by a double row of umbrella pines (Pinus pinea) and along Via Cilea, where scholastic facilities are located. The lot is an irregular polygon on flat ground measuring approximately 100 by 140 metres.

The curtain of umbrella pines along Via Wolf Ferrari is an important element. The project entails a parallel arrangement with setbacks and space reserved for the church forecourt. The parish complex responds to the fragmentary development of the neighbourhood by offering two public spaces: the church forecourt and an internal garden. The building converges its mass centrally and the portico provides a passage across the site, connecting the two public spaces and going all the way to Via Cilea. The complex is enclosed within a tuff wall and is composed of various volumes of differing heights. The nave, apse, bell tower and apartments emerge visually from the complex to establish a clear connection with the shopping centre on Via Wolf Ferrari through the cross-shaped opening that illuminates the main façade of the church. The use of lead as facing material emphasizes the volume of the apse. The various functional zones of the complex are arranged around the central portico. The south wing contains the church and the rectory with apartments for priests. To the north are the parochial offices and facilities. They are connected to the parish hall, which in turn connects to the surrounding neighbourhood. The forecourt is an inclined plane that slopes up toward the centre of the area and the entrance portico. At this central fulcrum, the perimeter walls come closer together and the building becomes thinner and permeable toward the inner garden. The portico roof, interrupted where it meets the façade, extends into the church. The rectangular plan of the central nave widens slightly toward the presbytery. The ferial chapel is located in the left-hand aisle, which leads to the sacristy and to the living quarters of the priests.

From its vertex at the front wall, the ceiling of the nave descends toward the presbytery. A blade of light separates the apse from the nave. The northern side of the apse rises vertically and receives natural light from a transverse elliptical window. With the exception of a side window near the atrium below the bell tower, the hall is illuminated exclusively with indirect natural light.

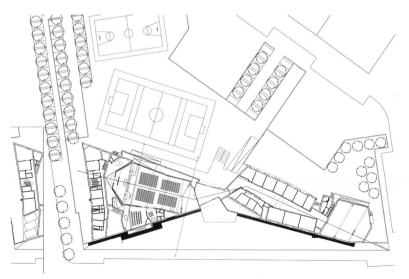

Left: ground floor plan.
Right: model seen from
the rear side and site plan.
Following pages: model
seen from the front
and elevations.

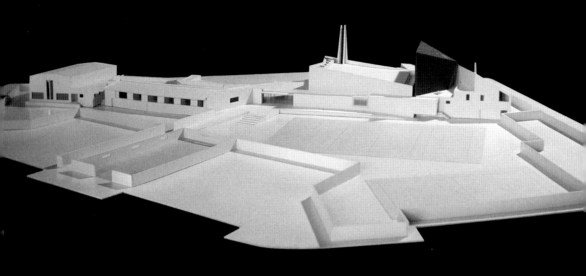
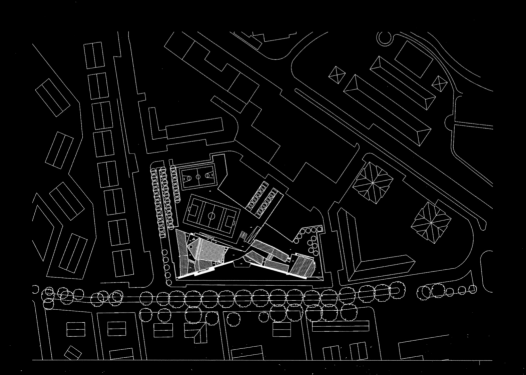

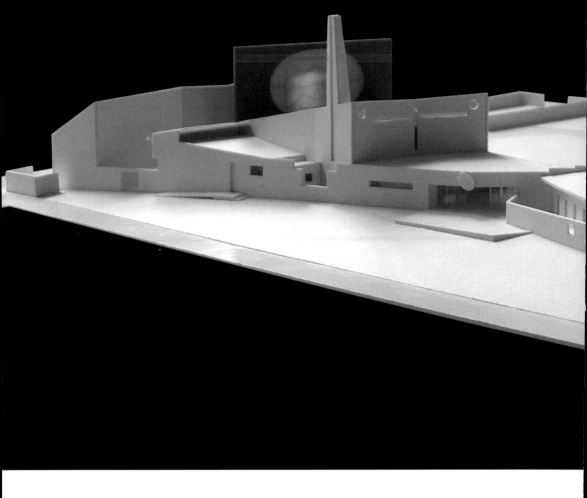

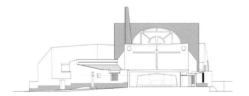

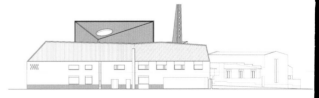

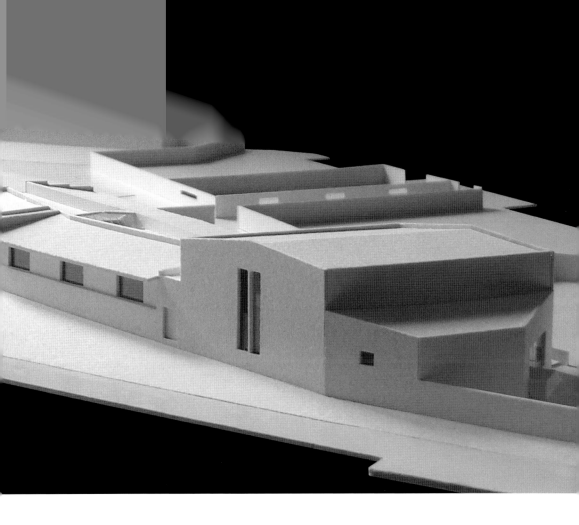

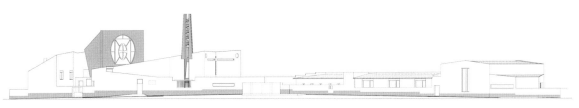

*The project descriptions
have been written by the
architects, and subsequently
edited by the author
of the volume.*

Credits

Rome Centre

**Richard Meier & Partners
Ara Pacis Museum**
Client
Municipality of Rome
Design team
Richard Meier, John
Eisler, Peter Burns,
Thibaut Degryse,
Simone Giostra,
Alfonso D'Onofrio,
Matteo Pericoli,
Hans Put, Michael
Vinh
*Project manager
in Rome*
Nigel Ryan
Audiovisual systems
Arch system srl
(Francesco Bianchi,
Giancarlo Bianchi)
Acoustical systems
Isotecnica AH Srl
(Andreas Hoeschein)
Curtain wall
I.B.M. (Michael Meyer)
Fountain
Eco-Tecno-Acqua
(M. Giovannoni)
Lighting
Fisher Marantz Stone,
ERCO Italia
Mechanical installations
Ove Arup & Partners
(conceptual phase),
Italprogetti (Gennaro
Stamatti), Costen srl
(Luca Grossi)
Structures
Guy Nordenson
(Conceptual phase),
Italprogetti
(Giorgio Caloisi,
Luciano Guerci)
Artistic direction
Richard Meier
Site directors
Dario Grasso, Marco Lozzi,
Sandro Getuli (safety)
General contract
Maire Engineering
Chronology
1995-2006

**Francesco Cellini
Remodelling of the
Mausoleo di Augusto
and Piazza Augusto
Imperatore**
Design team leader
Francesco Cellini
*Members of the design
team*
Mario Manieri Elia, Carlo
Gasparrini, Renato Nicolini,
Maria Margarita Segarra
Lagunes, Giovanni
Longobardi, Andrea
Mandara, Giovanni
Manieri Elia
Archaeologist
Dieter Mertens
Art historian
Elisabeth Kieven
Restoration
Maria Margarita Segarra
Lagunes
Landscaping
José Tito Rojo

**Juan Navarro Baldeweg
Bibliotheca Hertziana**
Clients
Max-Planck Gesellschaft
zur Foerderung der
Wissenschaften e.
V. München (Federal
Republic of Germany)
*Winning project in an
international tender*
Juan Navarro Baldeweg
(Madrid)
Recovery
Enrico Da Gai (Max Planck
Gesellschaft, München),
Paolo Riccetti (Municipality
of Rome)
*Definitive architectural
project*
Juan Navarro Baldeweg,
Enrico Da Gai (Rome)
*Executive architectural
project*
Juan Navarro Baldeweg,
Enrico Da Gai (collaborator)
Structures
Tekno IN ingegneri
associati (Rome)

Elevation structures:
Alberto Parducci, Alfredo
Marimpietri, Marco Mezzi
Foundations: Sergio Olivero
Mechanical installations
Tecnisches Büro - Franz
Steiner (Stuttgart)
Engineer Jaeger,
Mornhinweg + Partner
(Egna-BZ)
Electrical systems
Corrado Becucci (Rome)
Seti impianti (Rome)
Contractor
CCC Consorzio Cooperative
Costruzioni (Bologna)
Construction company
CDC Cooperative di
Costruzioni (Modena)
Site manager
Enrico Da Gai
*On site structural
certifications*
Maurizio Cagnoni

**Nemesi Studio
Museum Walkways
at the Mercati Traianei**
Client
Municipality of Rome
Project design
Nemesi Studio
Michele Molè (Team
leader), with Maria Claudia
Clemente and Daniele
Durante
Project team
Rossana Atena, Daniele
Durante, Federico Pitzalis,
Emiliano Roia, Adele Savino
Model
Niccolò Di Meglio
Structures
Paolo Iuliani
Installations
Architect Riccardo Fibbi
Construction company
Impresa Pasqualucci,
Rome
Chronology
Initiated: 1999
Conclusion: 2005
Cost
750,000 euros

**Carlo Aymonino
Museum Space
in the Campidoglio**
Client
Municipality of Rome,
Office for Cultural Heritage
(councillor
Eugenio La Rocca,
Director of the Musei
Capitolini Anna Mura
Sommella).
Directing official:
Maddalena Cima
Architectural project
Carlo Aymonino
with Maria Luisa Tugnoli,
Geneviève Hanssen,
Raffaella Castrignanò
Structures
Antonio Michetti,
Giuseppe Solvetti,
Marco Astolfi
Installations
Gianfranco Zamboni
Historical research
Alessandra Provenzali
Survey
Margherita Caputo
with Antonio Furgone
and Alessandro Sartor
(consultants)
Environmental impact
Marco Fano
Safety
Domenico Tocci
Lighting
Studio Associato
Annunziata e Terzi
(Adriana Annunziata,
Corrado Terzi)
with Silvia Felici
Installations
Francesco Stefanori
Director of works
Domenico Tocci
Contractor
Gherardi engineer Giancarlo
spa. Director of works:
Antonio Asta
Site management: Gerardo
Delfini
Surfaces and volumes
Sala di Marco Aurelio,
ex Giardino Romano:

795 mq, 6,925 mc
New surfaces which integrate those already existing (including the sala del Giardino Romano): 964 mq, 8,030 mc
Chronology
Project dated from 1993 executed: 2004-2005
Cost
4,559,912.80 euros

ABDR
Reconstruction of the ex Serra Piacentini at the Palazzo delle Esposizioni
Client
Municipality of Rome. Azienda Speciale Palaexpo
Team leader
ABDR
Design team
ABDR + S.A.C. Spa + IGIT
Collaborators
Architects Angela Arnone and Maria Persichella (general technical coordination), arch. Steffen Ahl, arch. Alessandra Gobbo, arch. Marta Petacco, arch. Alessio Scarale, arch. Giancarlo Vaccher
Structures
Mario Desideri, Odine Manfroni engineers
Consultants
Valerio Calderaro engineer (bioclimatic), Stefano Tiburzi (fire prevention)
Director of works
arch. Bruno Moauro, ing. Simona Coles, engineer
Contractor
S.A.C. Spa + IGIT
Functional surface
4200 mq
Chronology
2003-2004
Cost
15,000,000 euros

King Roselli Architetti ES Hotel
Project
King Roselli Architetti - Jeremy King, Riccardo Roselli
with Andrea Ricci, Claudia Dattilo (project leader) and Marina Kavalirek, Riccardo Crespi, Annalisa Bellettati
Property
C.R. INVEST s.r.l., Rome
Design coordination
Marzia Midulla Roscioli, Rome
Director of works
Nino Bazzi, Rome
General Contractor
ORION s.c.a.r.l., Rome (Gino Sbrizzi)
DICOS s.p.a., Rome (Piero De Bonis)
Acoustics
Biobyte srl, Milan (Enrico Moretti)
Structures
Dario D'innocenzo, Rome
Chronology
September 2000 - October 2002

5+1AA Remodelling of the ex Ferdinando di Savoia Barracks
Clients
Ministry for Infrastructure and Transport – Regional superintendent for public works of Lazio; Ministry for the Interior
Project
5+1AA (Alfonso Femia, Gianluca Peluffo) with Annalaura Spalla, Rome and Pierluigi Feltri (first lot)
Structures and installations
Paolo Cirillo, Rome
Surfaces
Section involved in the intervention: 28,000 mq
Gross functional surface

area: 43,840 mq
Gross over ground volume: 216,631 mc
Chronology
Preliminary project July 2001; definitive project 1st and 2nd lot (parts B and C) November 2001; definitive project 3rd lot (parts A and I) May 2001; definitive project 4th lot (parts D, E, F, H, L, M) November 2004; executive project 1st and 2nd lot July 2002; executive project 3rd lot February 2003; executive project 4th lot, assigned to an integrated contract, works initiated September 2002
Cost
48,326,000 euros

King Roselli Architetti Pontificia Università Lateranense Extension of the Pio IX Library
Client
Pontificia Università Lateranense (Rector, Monsignor Rino Fisichella)
Project and artistic direction
King Roselli Architetti Riccardo Roselli, Jeremy King, Andrea Ricci
Collaborators
Enrica Testi, Katia Scarioni, Giandomenico Florio, Arianna Nobile, Ulrich Grosse, Christina Hoffmann, Thabh-Truc Laura Duong, Toyohiko Yamaguchi
Structures
Proges Engineering (Andrea and Pierfrancesco Imbrenda)
Mechanical installations
Ovidio Nardi
Electrical installations
Donato Budano (CEM)
Director of works
Office of Technical services Governorate of the Vatican

State (Enrico Sebastiani; Roberto Pulitani assistant)
General contractor
C.P.C.
Tecnodir
Surfaces
New: 2000 mq
Chronology
Initiated: 2003
Construction initiation: 2004
Delivery: 2006

Rome Semicentre

The Office of Zaha Hadid MAXXI – Museo nazionale delle arti del XXI secolo
Client
Ministry for Cultural Heritage and activities
Project
The Office of Zaha Hadid
Design
Zaha Hadid and Patrick Schumacher
Local project director
Gianluca Racana
Tender project team
Ali Mangera, Oliver Domeisen, Christos Passas, Sonia Villaseca, Jee-Eun Lee, James Lim, Julia Hansel, Sara Klomps. Shumon Basar, Bergendy Cooke, Jorge Ortega, Stéphane Hof, Markus Dochantschi, Woody K.T. Yao, Graham Modlen, Jim Heverin, Barbara Kuit, Ana Sotrel, Hemendra Kothari, Zahira El Nazel, Florian Migsch, Kathy Wright, Jin Wananabe, Helmut Kinzer, Thomas Knuvener, Sara Kamalvand
Project team
Fabio Ceci, Paolo Matteuzzi, Anja Simons, Ana M. Cajao, Matteo Grimaldi, Mario Mattia, Maurizio Meossi, Luca Peralta, Barbara Pfenningstorff, Maria

Velceva, Paolo Zilli,
Gianluca Ruggeri,
Luca Segarelli
Partner studio
ABT (David Sabatello,
Piercarlo Rampini, Paolo
Olivi, Marco Valerio
Faggiani, Paolo Bisogni)
Structures
Anthony Hunt Associates
(Les Postawa)
OK Design Group (Simone
Di Cintio)
*Installations and electric
systems*
Max Fordham and Partners
(Henry Luker, Neil Smith)
OK Design Group
(Carlo Rossi, Pete
Fanelli, Domenico
Raponi)
Lighting
Equation Lighting (Mark
Hensman, Paolo Giovane)
Acoustics Paul Gilleron
Acoustic
(Paul Gilleron)
Chronology
Competition 1997

ABDR
Annibaliano B1
Metro Station
Type of tender
Integrated contract
Client
Roma Metropolitane -
Municipality of Rome
Process manager
Pietro Lattanzi, engineer
Director of works
Andrea Sciotti, engineer
Contractor
A.T.I. Consorzio RISALTO
(Group leader and mandate)
with MAIRE ENGINEERING
S.p.A. MAIRE LAVORI
S.c.a.r.l.-I.C.O.P. S.p.a.-
T.P.M. S.r.l. (Imprese
Mandanti Cooptate)
General project design
MAIRE ENGINEERING
S.p.A., ing. Vincenzo Testa
(head engineer)

*Architectural design and
consultancy*
ABDR Architetti associati,
Maria Laura Arlotti, Michele
Beccu, Paolo Desideri,
Filippo Raimondo with
Nicolas Cazzato, Giancarlo
Vaccher
Collaborators
Antonella Antonilli,
Emanuele Clementi, Marco
Thomas Piacentini, Marco
Riccobelli
Chronology
Initiated: 2005
Concluded: 2008

Odile Decq Benoît
Cornette Architectes
Urbanistes
MACRO – Museo d'Arte
Contemporanea
Client
Municipality of Rome
Project design
Odile Decq
with Burkhard Morass
Project team
Giuseppe Bavarese, Valeria
Parodi, Frédéric
Haesevoets, Stephane
Eggiman, Xavier Zanzen,
Christophe Bernard, Peter
Baalman
Consultants
Batiserf Ingenierie (France),
AI Engineering (Italia),
MB&Co (France)
Surfaces
Lot: 4,760 mq
Gross floor surface:
12,000 mq
Temporary exhibition
spaces: 2,480 mq
Services open to the public:
1,101 mq
Volume: 34,588 mc
Chronology
Tender: 2001
Project development:
2002-2004
Project execution: 2007
Cost
17,500,000 euros

ABDR
New Rome Tiburtina High
Speed Station
Direction of the project
was undertaken by all four
partners of studio ABDR
Maria Laura Arlotti, Michele
Beccu, Paolo Desideri
(Project leader), Filippo
Raimondo and the
architects Nicolas Cazzato
and Mauro Merlo from
the same studio.

• International design
tender
Client
Rete Ferroviaria Italiana Spa
Group leader
Prof. Paolo Desideri,
architect
Design team
ABDR Architetti Associati
Maria Laura Arlotti, Michele
Beccu, Paolo Desideri,
Filippo Raimondo
with: Nicolas Cazzato,
Mauro Merlo, Enzo
Calabrese (suspended
volumes)
Project management
Drees&Sommer Italia
Engineering, Massimo
Mazzocchi,
Busmann+Haberer
Architekten Deutschland
Collaborators
M. Abis, S. Ahl, A. Antonilli,
A. Arnone, G. Bellapadrona,
D. Binarelli, M. Cannarsa,
S. Cataldi, A. Ciocci,
E. Clementi, C. Del Colle,
V. Didier, M. Fiorentino,
L. Franco de Mendonça,
A. Fritzlar, A. Giglio,
A. Gobbo, T. Iazzetta,
G. Leoni, P. Mencacci,
M. Persichella,
T. Pescosolido, M. Petacco,
S. Pieretti, G. Pyckevet,
L. Salemi, A. Salvucci,
A. Scarale, B. Sepe,
L. Spanò, M. Tamburi,
G. Vaccher

Structures
Ezio Maria
Gruttadauria,Massimo
Majowiecki
Consultants
V. Calderaro (bioclimatic),
A. Desideri (geotechnical),
E. Mariotti (lighting design),
O. Manfroni (steel and
glass structures)
Functional surfaces
60,000 mq
Chronology
2001-2004
Cost
217,000,000

• Executive phase
Design
ABDR Architetti associati
Maria Laura Arlotti, Michele
Beccu, Paolo Desideri
(group leader), Filippo
Raimondo with: Nicolas
Cazzato, Mauro Merlo,
Giancarlo Vaccher
Coordination
Drees&Sommer Italia
Engineering, Massimo
Mazzocchi
Engineering
Proger s.p.a., F. Agresta,
M. Del Cimmuto, W.
Mauro (Coordination),
R. Massacesi (thermo fluid
systems), Dino Boni-
Manens Intertecnica s.p.a.
(electrical systems),
G. Ruggeri, S. Tiburzi (fire
prevention), M. Di Girolamo
(infrastructure)
Director of works
Rete Ferroviaria Italiana Spa
Work initiated
January 2006
Work concluded
December 2007

Labics
Città del Sole
Client
Parsitalia Real Estate
Project
Labics (Maria Claudia

Clemente, Francesco Isidori)
Tender project team
Susan Berardo, Leonardo Consolazione, Gaia Maria Lombardo, Giorgio Pasqualini, Laura Perri
Project development
Paola Bettinsoli, Chiara Capriulo, Gaia Maria Lombardo, Michele Morganti, Giorgio Pasqualini
Installation structures and sustainability consultants
3TI Progetti Italia
Programme
Underground car park, library, sales spaces, offices, residence
Overall surface
17,300 mq
Functional surfaces
13,500 mq
Chronology
2007-2010
Cost
35,43,709 euros

**Luciano Cupelloni
MACRO Future and Altra Economia at the Mattatoio**

• MACRO Future
Museo d'Arte Contemporanea Roma
Design and artistic direction
Luciano Cupelloni
Project design team
Risorse per Roma RpR Spa - Francesco Rubeo (technical director)
Massimiliano Di Martino (project director)
Paolo Grillo (structures)
Enrico Roberti, Franco Cipriani, Luigi De Marco, Erminio Ciccarella (installations)
Enrico Roberti (safety)
Alessandro Dellepiane (estimates)

Director of works
Luigi Caruso
Director of the Historical City Bureau
Gennaro Farina
MACRO Director
Danilo Eccher
Process director
Maurizio Marocco
Chronology
Project: July 2002 / July 2004
Evaluation process: October 2002
Initiated: August 2005
Conclusion: April 2007
Cost
2,000,000 euros

• Altra Economia
Project and Director of works
Luciano Cupelloni
Project design group
Luigi Sorrentino, Cesare Tocci (structures)
Ricerca & Progetto (bioclimatic and acoustic control)
Andrea Garasi, Federico Pacchieri (mechanical installations)
Francesco Cattaneo (electric systems and special installations)
Alessandro Dellepiane (estimates)
Collaborators
Marco Astolfi, Assunta Gaetani, Vincenzo Pasquariello, Marta Salvatore, Ricardo Soca Wiese, Lusilla Voci
Process manager
Mirella Di Giovine
Programme manager
Alessandro Messina
Chronology
Project: July 2004 / May 2005
Evaluation process: November 2004
Initiated: September 2005
Concluded: June 2007

Cost
4,500,000 euros

**Labics
Headquarters of Italpromo & Libardi Associati**
Client
Italpromo & Libardi Associati s.r.l.
Project design
Labics (Maria Claudia Clemente, Francesco Isidori, Marco) Sardella)
Project design team
Andrea Ottaviani, Magali Roig Liverato, Jun Sughimaru
Structures
Studio 3S – Camillo Sommese
Installations
Riccardo Fibbi, Carolina de Camillis
Surface area
1850 mq
Chronology
Project: 2002
Project execution: 2002-2004
Cost
1,500,000 euros

**OMA – Office for Metropolitan Architecture
Transformation of the Mercati Generali**
Client
The Mills Global Corporation
Area of the project
About 87,000 mq
Programme
About 250,000 mq; commercial, entertainment and cultural spaces
Partners in charge of the project
Rem Koolhaas and Ellen van Loon
Local architect
Roberto Otero
Project team
Kunle Adeyemi, Cristina

Murphy, Maurizio Scarciglia, Rob de Maat, Kees van Casteren, Gaspard Estourgie, Thomas v. Girsewald, Beatrice Schiavina, Berit Bessel, Beatriz Ramo, Marco di Piaggi, João Amaro, Ramona Jens, Tiago Simas Freire, Camia Young, Spela Stern, Frank Eittorf
Conservation consultants
B. Moauro and R. Capocaccia, Rome
Structures
Arup London, Arup Milan
Installations
Arup Amsterdam
Traffic
Arup London
Fire prevention / safety
Engineer Amaro, Turin
Landscape
Inside Outside, Amsterdam
Chronology
Competition: 2004
Completion: 2008
Cost
100-200,000,000 euros

**Giuseppe Pasquali, Alfredo Passeri
Rectorate, Faculty and Department of Law – Università Roma Tre**
Client
Università Roma Tre
Project design
Giuseppe Pasquali and Alfredo Passeri
Project team
E. Basile, L. Benedetto, D. De Gregori, G. Di Stefano and G.M. Verdone
Structures
Antonio M. Michetti, Lino Perfetti
Construction company
SAG srl Società Appalti Generali (D.L. Giampaolo Berti)
COSTINCEM srl (reinforced concrete structures)

VIBROSUD SpA
(Reinforced concrete
structures)
Chronology
Project: 1998
Conclusion of work: 2000
Cost
63,000,000 lire

**Sartogo Architetti
Associati
Church of Sacro Volto
di Gesù**
Client
Vicariato Opera Romana
per la Preservazione della
Fede e la Provvista di
Nuove Chiese in Roma
Project design
Sartogo Architetti Associati
- Piero Sartogo, Nathalie
Grenon
Structures
Antonio Michetti
Installations
Luigi Dell'Aquila
Director of works
Ignazio Breccia Fratadocchi
General contractor
Bianchini & Mancinelli
S.p.A.

**n! studio
Storehouse-Laboratory
at Villa dei Quintili**
Client
Archaeological
superintendence of Rome
Roma,
Person in charge of the
project Dr. Rita Paris
Project designers
Susanna Ferrini e Antonello
Stella Architetti Associati
n!studio
with Luigi Filetici
Collaborators
Claudia Farinelli,
Jutta Riehle
Structures
Salvatore d'Agostino
Director of works
Maria Grazia Fileticì,
Architect, Archaeological

Superintendence of Rome
Executing company
Officine Ragnini, Pitigliano
(Grosseto)
Cost
150,000 euros

**Massimiliano Fuksas
Centro Congressi Italia
at EUR**
Client
Municipality of Rome, EUR
SpA, CCI SpA
Project design
Massimiliano Fuksas
Engineering
A.I. Torino
Structures
Studio Majowiecki
Acoustics
Xu-Acoustique
Lot surface area
27.250 mq
Project surface area
51,000 mq
Building cubature
327,000 mc
Chronology
Tender for the first phase
November 1998; Tender for
the second phase February
2000; preliminary project
phase July 2001; Definitive
project February 2004;
Executive project May
2006; delivery of work April
2009
Cost
250,000,000 euros

Rome Outskirts

**Nemesi Studio
Church of Santa Maria
della Presentazione**
Client
Vicariato di Roma
Project
Nemesi Studio
Project leader
Michele Molè
Project team
F. Isidori, M.C. Clemente,
A. Savino, D. Durante,

M. Sardella, F. Cherchi,
A. Creti, F. Mammuccari,
R. Atena
Collaborators
Emiliano Roia, Giulia Andi,
Lorenza Giavarini,
Alessandro Ponzianelli,
Marco Bevilacqua, Andrea
Quagliola
Structures
G. Molè, C. Sommese
Installations
Riccardo Fibbi
General contractor
Ruggeri Costruzioni srl
Surfaces
4500 mq
Chronology
Tender: 1994
Project: 1995-1998
Execution: 1998-2002
Cost
3,100,000 euros

**Studio Valle Architetti
Associati
Shopping Centre
Porta di Roma**
*Urbanistic project
(1992-1997)*
Studio Valle Architetti
Associati: Gino Valle
with Piero Zucchi
and Alessandro Manaigo
*Architectural project
for a shopping mall*
Preliminary consultations
for the executive project,
Artistic direction Studio Valle
Architetti Associat:
Gino Valle (2000-2003),
Pietro Valle (2003-2006)
with Marco Carnelutti,
Walter Vidale and Ugo
Tranquillini
In collaboration with
Rossella Capri (Technical
office of Imprese Lamaro -
Project Manager)
Carlo Costantini
(for Ikea executive
development)
Fortebis srl (development
of the hotel-residence)

*Project and execution
of the Shopping Mall
Surface area*
Commercial:
150,000 mq
(Ikea 2 27,000 mq)
Hotel/residence:
7000 mq
Underground parking
facilities:
230,000 mq
Chronology
1992-1997

**Francesco Cellini
and Andrea Salvioni
Secondary School
in Casal Monastero**
Client
Municipality of Rome,
XII Department for Public
works and Urban
maintenance
Director: Maria Lucia Conti
Director of III U.O.: Roberto
Massaccesi
Process manager: Antonio
Giulio Ciocci
Project design
Francesco Cellini
and Andrea Salvioni
with Jana Kuhnle,
Caterina Aurora Rogai
Environmental consultant
Patricia Cristina Ferro
Pedagogical consultant
Roberto Maragliano
Structures
E.D.IN srl (Fabio Brancaleoni,
Marcello Colasanti)
Installations
3 TI progetti

**Garofalo Miura
Church of Santa Maria
Josefa**
Client
Vicariato di Roma
(Monsignor Gino Amicarelli,
Director of the New
Churches Office)
Project
Francesco Garofalo
and Sharon Yoshie Miura

Collaborators
Federico Cavalli, Simon
Hartmann
Model
Paul Blackmore
Structures
Antonio Michetti
Installations
Luigi Dell'Aquila
Construction company
Branchini e Mancinelli spa
Surface area
2300 mq
Chronology
Project: 1997-1998
Execution: 1999-2000
Cost
2,250,000 euros

IaN+
Tor Vergata University
Laboratories
Project design
Carmelo Baglivo, Luca
Galofaro, Stefania Manna
Chronology
Execution 2004

Italo Rota & Associati
Church of Santa
Margherita Maria
Alacoque
Client
Superintendence for public
works, Lazio region
Project
Italo Rota
with Fabio Fornasari,
Alessandro Perdetti,
Massimiliano Beltrami
Project team
Paolo Montanari,
Paolo Pasquini
Chronology
2000-2005

Architectuurstudio
Herman Hertzberger
School in Romanina
Client
Municipality of Rome,
VI Department for
programming and planning
policy of the Territory

of Rome, Capital city
Architectural project
Architectuurstudio Herman
Hertzberger
Project design team
Herman Hertzberger
with Cor Kruter, Dickens
van der Werff
Partner studio
Marco Scarpinato
Architetto
with Vincenzo Gagliardo,
Lorenza Majorana, Lucia
Pierro, Carmelo Vitrano
Consultants
Libera Dolci, Carlo Romano,
Francesco Nicolicchia,
Ariane Vervoorn
Models
Marijke Teijse, Wing Ung

Marco Petreschi
Defence Administrative
Centre in Cecchignola
Client
Ministry of Defence
Design project
Marco Petreschi with
the Direzione Generale
dei Lavori e del Demanio
(Geniodife)
Design team
Giulia Amadei
Massimo Sciarpa
(landscape)
Dario Parise (functional
project)
Graphic elaboration
Claudio Merler
Riccardo Toccaceli Trainelli

Monestiroli Architetti
Associati
Church of San Carlo
Borromeo
Project
Antonio Monestiroli,
Tomaso Monestiroli,
Massimo Ferrari
Client
Opera Romana per la
preservazione della fede
e la provvista di nuove
Chiese in Roma

Surface area of the lot
8,800 mq
Project surface area
2,700 mq
Chronology
Project for tender: 2005
Definitive project: 2006

Umberto Riva
Church of San Guglielmo
Project designers
Umberto Riva
with Giovanni Drugman,
Michele Pizzicato
Collaborators
Alessio Prestia,
Luca Spagnolo

Photographic Credits

Gabriele Basilico: pp. 22-23, 69

Hélène Binet: pp. 93-95

Santi Caleca: pp. 78 (small image), 79 (large immage and small image to the right)

Luca Casonato: pp. 26-27

Ernesta Caviola: pp. 82-83

Maddalena Cima: p. 63

Piero de Grossi: pp. 173

Oscar Ferrari: pp. 180-181

Luigi Filetici: pp. 59-61, 125-127, 155-159

Aldo Ippoliti: p. 15

Andrea Jemolo: cover, pp. 40-45, 67, 96-97, 100-101, 119, 139-141, 178

Jose King: p. 75

King Roselli: pp. 76-77, p. 78 (small images), p. 79 (small image to the left)

Rodolfo Migliari, Giulia Cupelloni: pp. 121-123, 123 (image at the bottom)

Alberto Muciaccia: pp. 133-137, 171-172

Valeria Paganini: pp. 64-65

UBIKmh: pp. 182-185

Aerial view of the airport of Urbe in the meander of the Tiber, near Castel Giubileo.

Sebastiano Brandolini

Sebastiano Brandolini graduated from the Architectural Association of London in 1982. From 1984 to 1996 he worked as editor and then chief editor of *Casabella*, and was responsible for the double issues on engineering, roads, and the United States. In 2003 he was a finalist for the Gold Medal in Architectural Criticism at the Milan Triennale. He has worked as an independent professional since 1990. In the period 1999-2003 (Studio Brandolini Valdameri), he designed and supervised the construction of airport and downtown offices for Hertz and a passive low energy house near Bergamo.

He collaborated on the design of three Entertainment Centres in northern Italy, drafted the Redevelopment Plan for the Burgo area in Corsico (near Milan), and was on the winning design team in the competition for the Palazzo del Cinema at the Venice Lido.

Since 1997 he has been a regular contributor of articles for the weekly *D-La Repubblica delle Donne* on current issues relating to architecture and urban transformation. He has written monographs on the Finnish studio Gullichsen Kairamo Vormala and on Alberto Ponis. His articles have appeared in a major publications such as *AA Files*, *Architecture*, *Arkkitehti*, *Bauwelt*, *Casabella*, *Costruire*, *Design Book Review*, *Domus*, and *The Architectural Review*. He is on the jury of the trans-border design prize 'Contemporary Alpine Architecture.'

He has held teaching posts at the Milan Polytechnic, the Venice IUAV, the London School of Economics, the Università Federico II of Naples, and the Ferrara School of Architecture.

In 2005, he published the volume *Milano. Nuova Architettura.*